CW00418188

The Qur'an Problem and Islamism

ALSO BY SALIM MANSUR

Delectable Lie: a liberal repudiation of multiculturalism

Islam's Predicament: Perspectives of a Dissident Muslim

The Indira-Rajiv Years: The Indian Economy and Polity 1966-1991 (with N. K. Choudhry, editors)

The Qur'an Problem and Islamism: *Reflections of a Dissident Muslim*

SALIM MANSUR

2017

Published by Mantua Books Ltd.
Canada
mantuabooks.com
Email: administration@mantuabooks.com

Copyright© 2017 Salim Mansur

No part of this book may be reproduced or transmitted in any form, by any means, electronic or mechanical, including photocopying and recording, information storage, and retrieval systems, without permission in writing from the publisher, except by a reviewer who may quote brief passages in a review or a writer quoting brief sections in a book on the same topic.

Library and Archives Canada Cataloguing in Publication

Mansur, Salim, author
The Qur´an problem and Islamism / Salim Mansur.

ISBN 978-1-927618-08-0 (softcover)

1. Islam--21st century. 2. Islamic renewal. 3. Qur´an--Criticism, interpretation, etc. 4. Islamic fundamentalism. 5. Islam and politics. I. Title.

BP161.3.M367 2017 297 C2017-907570-5

Cover Photograph by Salim Mansur

for Nina Rosenwald, a special friend,

&

for Yasmina *and* Inès, my dearest wife and daughter

Contents

Preface and Acknowledgements

In the felicitous phrase of Harold Isaacs, this book began as "scratches on our mind" on the subject of Islam and Muslims. At the end of the Cold War Islam and Muslims once again emerged as the hottest topic of concern for public discussion in the West. They became a threat for the West when Arabs of the desert first rode to war against the cross-bearing defenders of the Byzantine Empire in the early seventh century. As Maxime Rodinson remarked, "Western Christendom perceived the Muslim world as a menace long before it began to be seen as a real problem."[1] Norman Daniel discussed this history at length in his groundbreaking study *Islam and the West: The Making of an Image*.

During the Cold War decades in the twentieth century the West, led by the United States, viewed the Muslim world as a strategic asset and a partner in the effort to contain and defeat the Soviet Union and Communism. The priority of Cold War politics, however, made the West look aside or ignore the internal problems of the world of Islam, as Muslims struggled with the complexity of making the transition into the modern secular world of democracy. Then in the nineteen-eighties came the last fateful conflict of the Cold War fought against the occupying Soviet forces and their local allies in Afghanistan. With the assistance of Saudi Arabia and Pakistan, the United States armed and funded an army of Afghan *mujahideens* (freedom-fighters) and volunteers for *jihād* (holy war) poured in from across the Arab and Muslim world to join this decade long struggle that turned into, as Steve Coll described in his book on the Afghan conflict, the *Ghost Wars*. The Soviet forces in Afghanistan were defeated, Moscow withdrew its occupying forces, and subsequently Afghanistan became an inferno of tribal warfare.

The Muslim "holy warriors", as frontline soldiers in the war against Soviet communism in Afghanistan, morphed into "radical Islamist terrorists" that haunt us today—long after the Soviet Union itself has collapsed. We ignore the law of *karma*—of cause and effect, especially of unintended consequences—at our own peril, and the blowback from the Afghan war is yet to be exhausted.

The Afghan war was followed by the first Iraq war of 1991, the 1993 bombing of the World Trade Center in New York City, the Rwandan genocide, the wars in the Balkan, the Kosovo episode, the domino effects of failed states, as with the case of Somalia, and then the terrorist attacks planned and executed by al Qaeda warriors, on September 11, 2001. And with these horrific attacks against the United States the dormant image of Islam and Muslims as enemies of the West, and of modern civilization and democracy, was given new urgency. The West and the world of Islam are likely to remain caught up for some time in a state of asymmetrical conflict, even as the conflict within the world of Islam itself intensifies between those Muslims who seek to reconcile their faith and culture with the modern secular world, and those who fanatically reject this prospect.

In these pages I have sought to provide a perspective from within the world of Islam of the nature of the struggles among Muslims on the eventual outcome of which the future of more than a fifth of the world's population will depend. I am one among those Muslims who is at home in the West. I was born to an Indian Muslim family and raised in a traditional society that followed the Hanafi school of jurisprudence within the mainstream of majority Sunni Islam, and not unlike many Muslims in the West I am deeply aware of and sensitive to the culture and politics on both sides of the divide: the West and the world of Islam. It is from the perspective of an understanding of these two worlds and their misbegotten conflict that I seek to share my reflections as a dissident Muslim.

I mean by a "dissident Muslim" someone who either critically questions or rejects the "officially" sanctioned views, doctrines, and dogmas of traditional Islam in favour of "rethinking Islam" within the modern context as Mohammed Arkoun, the Franco-Algerian scholar of Islamic thought at the Sorbonne proposed. I also mean by "dissident" someone who is unwilling to be confined by any doctrine or groupthink, which seeks to limit man who is, as God or nature made him and as Hamlet opines, "infinite in faculty!" The Syrian poet and literary critic Ali Ahmed Said `Isbar, widely known by his pseudonym Adonis, remarked, "Man lights up everything, so how can he illumine if he is limited? From this point of view, *freedom is the essence of man*, and there is something infinite in man: it does not become less, nor can it be known completely and finally."[2] A "dissident" is instinctively a partisan of freedom and a "dissident Muslim" is someone whose understanding of Islam is not constrained by the weight of traditional consensus.

I owe a debt of gratitude to many who have supported me beginning with my parents, my siblings, and my partner in life, Yasmina, my son, Samir, and especially my daughter, Inès. I can never adequately return the love they have given me. I also owe a special debt of gratitude to my teachers who taught me the fundamentals to live a rewarding life.

And then there are those whose support made this book possible. I am thankful to David Galston of the SnowStar Institute of Religion in Ontario, Canada, for inviting me to speak about the Qur'an and Muhammad at an annual gathering of Christian pastors in Stratford, Ontario. Similarly, to Charles Asher Small for the invitation to speak on Muslim anti-Semitism at a seminar of the Institute for the Study of Global Antisemitism and Policy (ISGAP) held at McGill University in Montreal, Quebec. I am indebted to Nina Rosenwald of the Gatestone Institute in New York for publishing early versions of a few chapters in the book in the Institute's online journal, and to Howard Rotberg of Mantua

Books for having faith in my writings and assisting in publishing this book. I continue to remain indebted to that invaluable circle of friends—Munawar Karim, Joydeep Mukherji, Hasan Mahmud, Haytham Mahfoud, Raheel and Sohail Raza, Geoffrey Clarfield, Alan Perlmutter, Susan Cassan, Ron Posno, Fred Litwin, Rory Leishman, Syed Zahid Hussain, William Gairdner, Richard van Seters, Sudhir Handa, Irving Weisdorf, Adham Benni, Salma Siddiqui—with whom I have spent many wonderful hours discussing issues that went into this book and whose friendship I treasure. I also want to thank Bob Metz and Robert Vaughan of the Just Right Media in London, Ontario, for inviting me on a number of occasions while I was at work on this book to discuss Islam and Islamism with them on radio. And finally, I remain deeply indebted to Adrienne Dain for her editorial assistance. I am, however, responsible alone for any shortcomings or flaws in this book that a discerning reader may find.

~

Note for readers—When quoting the Qur'an throughout the book, except in chapter IV, I have quoted from A.J. Arberry's rendition in *The Koran Interpreted*. In chapter IV I have quoted from Muhammad Asad's rendition in *The Message of the Qur'an*. I also recommend for quick reference "an explanatory translation" (in the words of the translator) provided by Mohammed Marmaduke Pickthall in *The Meaning of the Glorious Koran*.

Introduction

In the era between the decline of antiquity and the dawn of modernity, that is, in the centuries designated in European history as medieval, the Islamic claim was not without justification... At the peak of Islamic power, there was only one civilization that was comparable in the level, quality, and variety of achievement; that was of course China. But Chinese civilization remained essentially local, limited to one region, East Asia, and to one racial group... Islam in contrast created a world civilization, polyethnic, multiracial, international, one might even say intercontinental.

Bernard Lewis[1]

In the sixteenth century of our era, a visitor from Mars might well have supposed that the human world was on the verge of becoming Muslim. He would have based his judgment partly on the strategic and political advantages of the Muslims, but partly also on the vitality of their general culture... In the sixteenth century, the Muslim peoples, taken collectively, were at the peak of their power, by the end of the eighteenth century they were prostrate.

Marshall G.S. Hodgson[2]

At the end of World War I the traditional order in the world of Islam, symbolized by the decadent and shrunken Ottoman Empire, collapsed in defeat. It was followed in 1924 by the decision of the Grand National Assembly of the Turkish people under Mustafa Kemal, their nationalist leader, to abolish the Caliphate based in Istanbul and send the last Caliph-Sultan Muhammad VI Wahid ud-Din into exile. With this decision an institution established by the companions of Muhammad, the Prophet of Islam, soon after his death in 632 was, it seemed to most Muslims, abruptly and unceremoniously annulled. Since its foundation, the Caliphate in theory had represented within majority Sunni Islam, as did the Papacy in the Roman Church, the central authority by the sanction of God's revealed Word. And Muslims, according to the *ulema* (religious scholars), owed obedience and loyalty to the Caliph as the supreme head of their religious and political community, the *ummah*.

Things fall apart, as the Irish poet William Butler Yeats wrote in "The Second Coming," when the center cannot hold and "mere anarchy is loosed upon the world." The abolition of the Caliphate meant for Muslims a falling apart of their traditional political order; it also meant that under the new circumstances of the modern world Muslims needed to engage in constructing a political order based on the idea of nation-states, or else to persist in maintaining the broken framework of the traditional order while holding on to the notion of the Caliphate. The history of political unrest and violence of the past century within the world of Islam might be explained as consequences of the collapse of the traditional order, since the idea of the Caliphate still appeals to a large segment of Muslims. As the world witnessed during this period, and more recently when Muslim terrorists belonging to the network of al-Qaeda founded by Osama bin Laden carried out the horrific attacks on September 11, 2001 in New York and Washington, that within this segment of the Muslim population there is a large pool of Muslims motivated by the idea of *jihād* (holy war), and readily drawn to violence and terror in their effort to resurrect the institution of the Caliphate. This war within Islam has the potential to rage indefinitely into the future so long as enough Muslims, driven by their nostalgia for the Caliphate and what it represents in their minds in terms of religion and politics, resort to violence in contesting the legitimacy of those holding power in Muslim majority countries.

But there is another explanation for wars within Islam, and it is as old as historical Islam. There is a strain of violence embedded in the history of Islam, which has its origin in tribalism and which has persisted into the present age; moreover, this strain of violence in the history of Islam right from the outset found support in those verses of the Qur'an that called upon the Prophet and his followers to fight those non-believers who waged war against them. Most Muslims remain in denial of this history. As the Prophet lay dying in Medina in the year 11 A.H. (*anno hegira*) of the Islamic calendar, there erupted among his immediate companions quarrels over the issue of succession, of who among them would assume leadership of the newly-minted community of Muslims as his deputy and successor (*khalif*, or Caliph) and, as a result, the seeds of wars that followed his death were sown.

The twenty-three years of Muhammad's career as the Prophet, according to Muslim belief, constitute the sacred history of Islam when "heavenly forces" supported him—just as Moses and his people, as told in the Hebrew Bible, were guided by days and by nights with "heavenly signs" to escape from their captivity in Egypt and into the Promised Land—to prevail over the pagan opposition. During the first twelve years of his prophetic career Muhammad preached Islam in his native city of Mecca, appealing to Meccans to listen to the Word of God revealed to him, abandon idol worship, and treat justly the poor, the weak, the orphans among them. But he was repeatedly abused and eventually forced to flee into exile under threats of death. He found refuge in Yathrib, later named *Madinat-un-Nabi* or the City of the Prophet, and referred since simply as Medina. In the remaining eleven years of his prophetic career Muhammad made his home in Medina, and at the head of his followers successfully fought and defeated the opposition of the Meccan confederacy in establishing Islam over pagan idolatry.

In modern terminology, the wars Muhammad fought were "wars of necessity" imposed on him and his movement by pagan Arabs. These wars were existential in nature, since if Muhammad had been decisively defeated in any one of the several encounters it would have meant his certain death, and "curtains" on the history of Islam, as we have known it. Muhammad's triumph over pagan Arabs was providential, hence unique, in opening a new chapter in world history under the heading of "Islam", alongside other chapters under the headings of Buddhism, Confucianism, Christianity and many other faith-traditions, in a world of competing civilizations with their origins no *less* providential than that of Islam. The Qur'an states:

> To every one
> of you We have appointed a right way
> and an open road.
> If God had willed, He would have made you
> one nation; but that He may try you
> in what has come to you. So be you forward
> in good works; unto God shall you
> return, all together; and He will tell you
> of that whereon you were at variance (5:50).

The history of Islam and Muslims, or *historical Islam*, after Muhammad might be described in terms such as *interest*-driven and, hence, *opportunistic*, not unlike the history of other faith-traditions and different only in terms of ethnicity and cultural patterns specific to the circumstances of each people. The unfolding of *historical Islam*, which followed the twenty-three years of Muhammad's prophetic mission as the *sacred history of Islam*, begins with the first generation of Muslims—the Arabs of the desert—successfully exploiting the weaknesses of the two neighbouring empires, the Persian and the Byzantine, which were exhausted by their wars. According to Ali Ahmed Said `Isbar, or known by his pseudonym Adonis,

> The death of the Prophet Muhammad was followed by the founding of the first caliphate and the transformation of Islam into a political regime. Religion itself was used in power struggles. The people, who were 'one' around the Prophet, experienced division, discord and war. Islam thus became an ideological war, and the Qur'an was interpreted according to these conflicts of interest. This is how the culture of *hadīth* and *al-ijmā`* (consensus) came into existence.
>
> The Islam of today is this historical Islam.[3]

This history of Islam and Muslims, or historical Islam, beginning in the fourth decade of the seventh century, has been profane and temporal, rather than sacred and providential, and it evolved dialectically in response to pressures and counter-pressures of rival cultures and civilizations.

Islam, as Frithjof Schuon in *Understanding Islam* remarked, did not invent strife, nor will it eliminate strife in the world. Strife resides in the heart of man (in Arabic *insan*, a generic term), as does peace. The heart represents, in the Islamic tradition, the seat of man's conscience and intellect; it is a mirror, according to the Sufis or the mystics of Islam, which when polished reflects the divine light. It is for man to locate the source of strife within his heart, remove the rust (the filth of a misdirected self) accumulated over it, polish it through prayers and remembrance of the One, and thus "unveiled", the heart of man becomes a mirror illuminated by the Light of the Ever-Compassionate and Ever-Benevolent One, known by whatever name addressed: in English called "God", in Hebrew "HaShem", in Arabic "Allah", in Sanskrit and Hindi "Bhagavan", in Bengali "Ishwaar", in Persian and Urdu "Khoda", in French "Dieu", etc.

The paths leading to God, according to the Sufis, are as many as there are those seeking Him. But individuals on these paths are unequal in their efforts, unequal in the self-knowledge, devotion, and humility needed on the path, and unequal in polishing and unveiling their hearts. There is a popular saying among the Sufis that there are many faces of Islam, as there are Muslims; but the truth in Islam and the truth of Islam is singular—there is only the one God, the Eternal and Absolute Reality, and every thing else believed and worshipped as god is unreal and false.

For the mystics of Islam, God is "neither this, nor that"; in other words, God is essentially beyond definition, since defining God would be limiting the illimitable. Similarly, the idea that there are many faces of Islam, as there are Muslims, suggests no one definition of Islam is adequate, unless Islam is defined simply as monotheism in terms of the Muslim article of faith—*lā ilāha illā-Llāh* ("There is no god, but God"). It follows a Muslim is someone who *submits* or *surrenders* to God, and only God knows the *true* quality of a "surrender" reflecting an individual's understanding of the cosmological reality of God and creation being One. The better meaning of "surrender" in this context is when an individual knowingly and voluntarily on comprehending the evidence "concedes" to the objective fact or reality before him, instead of resorting to a passive resignation indicative of "fatalism". The Qur'an states, "No compulsion is there in religion" (2:256), and in the act of surrender without coercion a free individual, as a believer, indicates unsullied acknowledgement of God. The effect of this voluntary surrender, as the Sufis testify, is attaining peace with the world willed by God. Johann Wolfgang von Goethe expressed this notion of Islam as follows:

> *How strange that in every special case*
> *one praises one's way!*
> *If Islam means "surrender into God's will"*
> *It's in Islam that we all live and die.*[4]

The ideal of Islam, as Goethe understood, stands apart from the reality of historical Islam. It is about the relationship between man and God, and between God and man. The archetype of this relationship is represented in the Biblical story of Abraham re-told in the Qur'an. In the Islamic tradition, Muslims revere Abraham as *Ibrahim Khalīlullāh* (or Abraham, the friend of Allah), and Hebron with the Patriarch's Tomb (or the Cave of Machpelah to Jews) is known in Abraham's honour as *al-Khalil* (the "friend") in Arabic.

Historical Islam, on the contrary, is the mundane history of Muslims, Arabs and non-Arabs. It was historical Islam unfolding in the seventh century proximate to the mundane reality of the eastern half of Christendom, or the Byzantine Empire, which made for enmity and conflicts between the two faith-traditions.

Historical Islam was expansive in the making of *Dār al-Islam* (House of Islam), and the resulting wars with Christendom were unavoidable. If physical distance had separated Christendom and *Dār al-Islam,* as Christendom was physically set at distance from the faith-traditions of the East—Hinduism, Buddhism, Confucianism, Taoism—the conflicts between Christianity and Islam, and Christians and Muslims, would have been improbable. But the burden of this history shaped the mutual perceptions of both Christians and Muslims, and it has persisted into the deadly quarrels of our contemporary politics.

Muslims in general conflated their mundane history with the ideal of Islam, and partly from fear of political violence submitted to individuals who usurped power by claiming legitimacy as successors to the Prophet. The usurpation of power and the mechanics of legitimizing it on the basis of the Qur'an and on the authority of the Prophet—when both of these sources are unclear and open to debate, as have been the case since the first schism in historical Islam that led to the massacre of Hussein, grandson of Muhammad, and members of his family and followers in Karbala, Iraq, in 680[5]—laid the template of violence that has characterized the political culture of Muslims ever since. Consequently, the ever-lurking fear of wars within Islam, or Muslim-on-Muslim violence, has provided the motive and rationale to religious scholars (*ulema*) and jurists (*fuqāha*) of Islam ever since to readily offer doctrinal support to tyrants as a preventive measure against anarchy.

While the strain of violence has been a prominent leitmotif embedded in historical Islam, the early centuries of this history were also illustrative of the Muslim capacity to innovate and imitate in the making of Islamic civilization. But this capacity was dealt a lethal blow by the populist reaction of the literal-minded followers of Abul Hasan al-Ash`arî (d. 935) against speculative philosophy and free-thinking rationalism of those identified as Mu`tazilîs. Ash`arîsm and Ash`arîtes after al-Ash`arî represented the Arab reaction against Mu`tazilîs among whom Muslims of non-Arab origin numbered more than ethnic Arabs.

The fatal crippling of Islamic culture and civilization can be traced back to the defeat of the Mu`tazilîs. In his *History of Western Philosophy* Bertrand Russell remarked,

> Philosophy, as I shall understand the word, is something intermediate between theology and science. Like theology, it consists of speculations on matters as to which definite knowledge has, so far, been unascertainable; but like science, it appeals to human reason rather than to authority, whether that of tradition or that of revelation. All *definite* knowledge—so I should contend—belongs to science; all *dogma* as to what surpasses definite knowledge belongs to theology. But between theology and science there is a No Man's Land, exposed to attacks from both sides; this No Man's Land is philosophy.[6]

In forbidding speculative philosophy the authorities, specifically among the majority Sunni Muslims, chose theology over science and ruled that dogma cannot be subjected to human reason. There was no mandate for such a ruling in the Qur'an, nor could it be inferred on the basis of any credible logic that the Prophet may have made a pronouncement, however remote, for which there was no basis in the Qur'an and that nevertheless would provide justification for forbidding philosophy. In prohibiting philosophy, the rulers, in connivance with the religious scholars, fenced off the No Man's Land where individuals could freely speculate on the nature of the material world and the mystery of its origin—including Aristotle's reference to the Unmoved Mover. The Qur'an, on the contrary, commands, "And say, 'O my Lord, increase me in knowledge" (20: 114). The result of forbidding speculative philosophy, however, was turning off the light of creative thinking among Muslims in general—or, as Robert Reilly has described it in his book *The Closing of the Muslim Mind*—and in effect making the "House of Islam" a citadel of opposition to the emergent modern world and modernity.

There is undeniably a hunger among a growing segment of the Muslim population for Islamic reforms, which hopefully might bridge the gap between the world of Islam and the modern world of science and democracy. But there is uncertainty about what is meant by "Islamic reforms", and this uncertainty fuels disagreement among Muslims, igniting a violence that is embedded in historical Islam. If "Islamic reforms" are to mean anything substantively positive then at a minimum Muslims will need to insist on and defend their rights to free-thinking, to appeal to human reason against the weight of traditional dogma, to revive once again the spirit of the Mu`tazilîs and reject the literal-mindedness of the ruling orthodoxy that produced the deadening culture of historical Islam. The prerequisite for the success of any reform sought by Muslims that could advance their world on the path for science and democracy is, I believe, how well they understand the difference between the *ideal* of Islam and *historical* Islam—the former is transcendent and eternal, while the latter is mundane and temporal—and that nothing relating to historical Islam, including Shariah or the Islamic law, is closed to reform and, therefore, to change, provided there is sufficient will among Muslims to change their world.

In 2017 the five-hundredth anniversary of Martin Luther sending a letter to his superiors with his 95 theses—in which he spelled out the doctrine of "justification by faith", and which in retrospect was a spark that roused a restless Christendom to the wars of the Reformation and Counter-Reformation in the making of modern Europe and the West—the Muslim world lies stricken and torn asunder by the wars within Islam. The post-World War I Middle East between the Nile and the Fertile Crescent has imploded, and the wars of the early twenty-first century in Iraq and Syria have disclosed to the world that the capacity of man to do evil is not bound in time or in space, and illustrate the permanence of evil in human history. The world of Luther lies in the past, but what made that world a tinderbox set to go up in flames as it did, resided in the heart of man, and is ever present. Europe and Christendom emerged from the Dark and the Medieval Ages and from their horrors, but not entirely. The history of Europe and the West since Luther is pockmarked with wars, inquisitions and terror, revolutionary and counter-revolutionary violence, anti-Semitism, pogroms, racism, the Holocaust, gulags, and world wars. But this list of human depravity is one column in the ledger of the West's history, while in the other column is the list of the West's triumphs as testimony to its human ingenuity and goodness. The story of Europe and the West is a reminder of what is forgotten during the times of duress: that man is the author both of his fortune and misfortune. The story of historical Islam in general differs from that of the West in particular details, but not in substance, for it is the story of peoples, of Muslims, belonging to one human family.

I.

Islam and Islamism

Islam did not invent strife; the world is a constant disequilibrium, for to live means to struggle...The practice of Islam, at whatever level, is to repose in effort; Islam is the way of equilibrium and of light which comes to rest upon that equilibrium.

Frithjof Schuon[1]

Islam is a revolutionary concept and a way of life, which seeks to change the prevalent social order and remould it according to its own vision. Based on this definition, the word 'Muslim' becomes the name of an international revolutionary party that Islam seeks to form in order to put its revolutionary programme into effect. Jihad signifies that revolutionary struggle involving the utmost use of resources that the Islamic party mobilizes in the service of its cause.

Sayyid Qutb[2]

Thus We appointed you a midmost nation that you might be witnesses to the people, and that the Messenger might be a witness to you.

The Qur'an, 2:143

Since September 11, 2001 the West has been confounded with the question whether Islam and Islamism are one and same, or if there is a critical distinction to be drawn between the two. How this question is answered has serious implications for understanding and explaining the immense convulsion inside the Muslim world.

Islamism is an ideology fascistic and totalitarian in impulse and action, masquerading as religion. The proponents, advocates, activists and apologists of Islamism, irrespective of whatever guise these Islamists assume in public, are engaged in the sort of radical politics the West became acquainted with in the early decades of the twentieth century with the rise of Communism, Fascism and Nazism.

Islamism is about power: Islamists are obsessed with power to the extent that such obsession becomes pathology. The political mission of Islamists is to establish a Shariah-based state, idealized as the only true and genuine expression of Islam. Abul A'la Maududi, the founder of Jamaat-i-Islami in South Asia, was blunt about his Islamism. Maududi insisted that Islam was a fully formed and coherent political system best described as "kingdom of God" or "theo-democracy"—entirely unrelated to the idea of democracy as understood in the West. The plainspoken purpose of the Jamaat is to train and prepare a cadre of Islamist Muslims to acquire or seize political power and establish a totalitarian state. "In such a state," Maududi wrote, "no one can regard any field of his affairs as personal and private. Considered from this aspect the Islamic State bears a kind of resemblance to the Fascist and Communist states."[3]

The Arab counterpart to the Jamaat is the Muslim Brotherhood; its founder, Hasan al-Banna, and its leading theorist, Sayyid Qutb, similarly described the objective of their movement as *jihād*, or the struggle to establish by force a Shariah-based state. Such a state, consistent with their ideological presuppositions, would be by necessity totalitarian. For Maududi, al-Banna, Sayyid Qutb and their followers, political sovereignty belongs to God, the Qur'an is their constitution, and political authority is legitimated by religious scholars, the *ulema*. In the streets of the Muslim world, the popular motto of the Muslim Brothers (*al-Ikhwān al-Muslimīn*)—"Allah is our objective. The Prophet is our leader. The Quran is our law. Jihad is our way."—expresses the program, the activism and the goal of political mobilization, which are uniformly directed toward securing control of total power.

Hence Islamism, loosely defined, is the politics of theocracy, and Islamists are theocrats. Here we might note Albert Camus's warning: "Politics is not religion, or if it is, then it is nothing but the Inquisition."[4] Maududi, al-Banna and Qutb were ideologues influenced by the radical and revolutionary politics of their time: the emergence of fascist Italy, Nazi Germany and the communist Soviet Union; similarly, Khomeini of Iran, as their contemporary, was influenced by the same developments in Europe.

Islam, on the contrary, is a faith-tradition. The central message or foundational principle, as revealed in the opening chapter of the Qur'an, is the appeal to man, made by Muhammad, to worship One God, the God of Abraham, and to live earnestly in awareness of the Day of Reckoning when individuals will be answerable for their deeds. In other words, Islam is essentially about man's relationship with God, and how it ideally informs him about his place in the world.

Islam in history is multi-dimensional; and though politics is one of the dimensions, it cannot usurp entirely other dimensions of man's non-political and spiritual longing in this world. Shariah, or the Islamic legal code derived from the Qur'an and the traditions of the Prophet, is a human construct, limited and fallible as is any human endeavour stamped by the limitations of the epoch in which it was worked out. Islam, a religion, cannot, therefore, be turned into a handmaiden of politics, or squeezed into a political ideology, or reduced to the restrictions of the Shariah devised in the early middle age; and when this occurs, Islam is turned into Islamism.

Islamists insist Islamism *is* Islam. Anti-Islamist or non-Islamist Muslims reject such reductionism. The Islamist version of the Islamic order on display, established in the early decades of the twentieth century—ironically with the assistance of Western powers—is the Saudi Kingdom. It was a political marriage between a Bedouin tribe and the Wahhabi sect that was, since its inception in the eighteenth century until it emerged triumphant in the twentieth, a marginal, extremist, sectarian, even vulgar, movement regularly held in check by the Caliph of Islam and the mainstream Sunni Muslim rulers of the Ottoman Empire. The other more recent example is the Shi'ite Islamic Republic of Iran, founded by Ayatollah Khomeini.

At the center of the current convulsion in the Muslim world, or Islamdom, as in Turkey and Egypt, is the contest between Islamists and anti-Islamists, between theocrats and anti-theocrats. This contest is hugely complicated by the turmoil that inevitably accompanies the transition of societies and cultures from pre-modern to modern. Here, the relevant analogy to explain this convulsion within Islamdom is to recall Christendom's long, tortuous, immensely bloody and violent transition in the making of the modern world. This is the history of the past 500 years, from the Inquisition through to the end of the Cold War.

Islamism is an aberrant strain of Muslim thinking that can be traced back in the Arab-Muslim history to the earliest years of Islam. Its defining characteristic is intolerance of others, including Muslims, and glorification of violence against all who disagree with the Islamist rendition of Islam. It might be said that the earliest expression of Islamism in Arab-Muslim history is embedded in the horrific crimes of murder of the members of the Prophet's family: his cousin and son-in-law Ali, the fourth Caliph; and then the massacre of the Prophet's grandson, Hussein, with his male companions and family members in Karbala in modern Iraq. But it was only in the past century, when Muslim societies emerged as independent states following the two world wars of the twentieth century, that Islamism came to be formulated as a political ideology of counter-revolution against the liberal and secular values that first emerged in Europe in the making of the modern world. Islamism, it might be said, is the ideology of Muslim opposition to modernity.

For the West, the imperative in distinguishing between Islam and Islamism, since at least September 11, 2001, is about working out the appropriate and relevant response to the political-military threats of Islamism and the ambitions of Islamists. This would be a response for containing Islamism and assisting over the long haul the effort of anti-Islamist Muslims to modernize their societies; it could be akin to the response conceived by George Kennan, the American diplomat and State Department official, soon after the Second World War ended, to contain Soviet Communism and assist those within the boundaries of Soviet control to acquire freedom.

If Islamism is Islam, as some in the West insist, then it logically follows that the West is at odds with all Muslims without there being any need to make distinctions among them, and Islam itself is the threat to the West as a civilization. This would mean that the West and the Muslim world are at war; that Islam is monolithic and the notion of anti-Islamist Muslims is absurd as none exists; and that any sort of engagement with the Muslim world and its population approaching two billion on the basis of coexistence is foolish, as Muslims without exception, openly or through dissembling, seek the destruction of the West. It is not surprising that such a view is the flip side of the deadly insistence by Islamists that non-Muslims, without exception, are infidels; that Muslims opposed to Islamism are heretics and apostates, and that their Islamist struggle, the global *jihād*, is the genuine face of Islam in carrying out God's mandate of establishing Shariah-based rule everywhere.

If Islamism is genuinely Islam then the question follows: why is it that so many Muslims repudiate the assertion of Islamists and, despite immense risks, continue to resist the theocrats in their midst? Why is it that in huge numbers—for instance, the many millions as we have seen in the streets of Cairo and other Egyptian cities; or in Tunisia; or in Istanbul and elsewhere in Turkey; or in Dhaka and towns across Bangladesh in support of guilty verdicts handed down in trials of members of Jamaat-i-Islami indicted for crimes against humanity during the nation's liberation war of 1971; or the near total rejection of Islamist religious parties repeatedly in national elections in Pakistan; or the support of Iranians, especially the young voters, for anti-establishment politicians in presidential elections, as in 2009—Muslims reject Islamism as authoritarian, supremacist, misogynistic, and a violent perversion of Islam?

Any objective and impartial analysis of the convulsions in the Muslim world, as the ones described as "Arab Spring" in the Middle East and North Africa, will find that in the midst of all the difficulties of poverty, corruption, underdevelopment, cultural backwardness, economic stagnation, military misrule, ethnic and sectarian divisions, gender inequality and misogyny, there is the deep division among Muslims on how they understand Islam and their place in the world as Muslims. It is this almost irreconcilable divide between Islamist Muslims and anti-Islamist Muslims that exacerbates all other divisions of class, sect, and ethnicity across Islamdom or the Muslim world.

The simple fact is that Islam and Islamism are not one and the same. Islamism as a totalitarian ideology is a perversion of Islam. Muslims are engaged in a historic struggle, just as Christians were once, in striving to reconcile revelation and reason; in separating religion from politics; in acknowledging the place of philosophy and science in the making of the modern world; in coming to terms with the imperatives of democracy and individual rights, and protecting freedom of religion and freedom of conscience equally for everyone irrespective of their belief, ethnicity, or gender. What is at play is the not-so-pleasant, complex reality of reform—of the historic transition of Muslim societies and cultures, from pre-modern into the modern world. It is a reminder for those who have forgotten, or never learned, how bitterly fought was Christendom's transition, stretched out over several centuries.

The conflict inside the Muslim world might ultimately be characterized as one between tyranny and freedom, even if that tyranny is packaged in God's name by those claiming to be His representatives irrespective of whether they are imams, sheikhs and ayatollahs, or political parties and movements such as the Jamaat, the Brotherhood, the Taliban, the Hamas, or the Hezbollah. In this conflict the West cannot afford to be neutral, and in supporting freedom, even when it is driven by self-interest, the choice for the West is not overly difficult or complicated. The strategically right thing to do is provide moral and material assistance to Muslims struggling against Islamists. It requires, therefore, making the distinction between Islam and Islamism, of recognizing anti-Islamist Muslims as allies, and acknowledging that the West together with anti-Islamist Muslims oppose Islamism and Islamists in their global *jihad* against freedom loving people everywhere. It also requires the West to remain true to its own ideals and values, acquired through much sacrifice in blood and treasure, and to be guided by them in order to assist anti-Islamist Muslims wisely. It is vital the West maintains its moral authority while assisting anti-Islamist Muslims during what inevitably will be a long and arduous struggle, and also that it remains true to the ideals of freedom and democracy in order to effectively assist Muslims in their struggle to reconcile Islam with modernity.

II.

On the Historical Muhammad

> *Muhammad is naught but a Messenger; Messengers have passed away before him.*
>
> The Qur'an, 3:144.

> *Muhammad is not the father of any one of your men, but the Messenger of God, and the Seal of the Prophets; God has knowledge of everything.*
>
> The Qur'an, 33:40.

> *By the Pen, and what they inscribe, thou are not, by the blessing of thy Lord, a man possessed.*
>
> The Qur'an, 68:2.

Albert Schweitzer's memorable book, *The Quest of the Historical Jesus: A Critical Study of Its Progress from Reimarus to Wrede*, was first published in 1906. It was a landmark event in religious studies and since then scholarly inquiry into historical Jesus became a major area of scholarship. Why was the Jesus of the New Testament—the Jesus of Matthew, Mark, Luke, and John—not sufficient for learning about the central iconic figure of Christianity? The answer to such a question, as John Dominic Crossan provided, was the "gospels are, in other words, interpretations. Hence, of course, despite there being only one Jesus, there can be more than one gospel, more than one interpretation".[1]

There is no similar inquiry into the "historical Muhammad" as an area of research among Muslims. For such an inquiry would suggest there is some variance between what we might know of Muhammad on the basis of modern historiography and what we know of Muhammad through traditional Muslim sources as the

Prophet of Islam. In the first instance our knowledge of Muhammad would depend upon the reliability of sources, upon treating these sources with the due scepticism required for scientific understanding of the subject, and that such knowledge would rest upon historical objectivity and independent criticism. In the second instance our knowledge of Muhammad as a prophet revered by Muslims rests upon the collective memory of Muslims as a faith community (the *ummah*), and this memory has been enriched by re-telling from one generation to another as a sacred story that cannot be subjected to critical study for fear of insulting the Prophet and his community of faithful. In a nutshell this is the problem when attempting to write or speak about Muhammad as a historically reliable figure distinct from Muhammad revered and venerated by Muslims as their Prophet.

But this problem is not unique in respect to what we know about Muhammad as a founder of a world religion. The problem is about the same when it comes to what we know as historically reliable about Moses or Buddha or Jesus. Indeed, very little. With the discovery of the Dead Sea Scrolls in 1947 the historicity of Jesus came to be questioned, yet these texts written by members belonging to a Jewish community, the Essenes, over two thousand years ago did not irreparably undermine Christian belief in Jesus as divine. The problem, however, varies. Modern historiography may bring discomfort to Jews, Buddhists and Christians, but such discomfort in our time in the early decades of the twenty-first century is not raised to a level of anger or rage that might turn lethal against those engaged in the critical study of religious history. In the case of Muhammad, however, to bring modern historiography to inquire into his historicity is to risk the wrath of a great many Muslims. It is a peril that only the foolhardy will dismiss or ignore given the evidence of the Rushdie affair, the Danish cartoon controversy, the *Charlie Hebdo* shooting in Paris, and physical threats of violence against those who could be seen as insulting Islam's Prophet and Muslims who revere him.

There is one thing that most people, Muslim or non-Muslim, interested in Islam as religion, culture, or politics will agree upon. This is Muhammad's place in history. Few will dispute his importance, if not greatness. History is retrospective judgment, and a biography of a great individual is a retrospective judgment on his career and what his life has meant in giving shape to the lives of other people for good or for ill. In writing about the craft of history Jacob Burckhardt, the nineteenth century Swiss historian of cultures, devoted some thought to great men and greatness in history. He wrote,

> The great man is...a man without whom the world would seem to us incomplete because certain great achievements only became possible through him in his time and place and are otherwise unimaginable. He is an essential strand in the great web of causes and effects. "No man is irreplaceable," says the proverb. But the few that are, are great.[2]

Muhammad was such a man, as were Moses, Buddha and Jesus. But in Muhammad's case, perhaps much more so than in the lives of the other three great men as founders of religions, his life came to be seen in retrospect by his followers as one fused with or indistinguishable from Islam as religion and as civilization. Long after Muhammad had passed away, his favourite wife Ayesha was asked by his followers to attest to his moral character. Ayesha responded, as recorded in the traditions of the Prophet, "His moral character was the Qur'an." Hence, the testimony of a wife who knew the Prophet most intimately indicated his character was sublime and irreproachable. It also meant that since the Qur'an was taken on faith by Muslims to be the Word of God, they came to believe that the individual through whom God's Word was revealed to humankind was by necessity sublime and fault-less. Out of such testimonies, and these over time were woven into a vastly intricate tapestry of narratives by Muhammad's followers, the few known facts of his life dissolved in the myth that grew around his person. It was this myth as sacred literature that Muslims built into a protective wall around Muhammad as Prophet, and any indulgence shown in questioning that myth in whole or in part was considered insulting. Hence, the cautionary words, "Be careful with Muhammad," spread beyond the Muslim world into the West.

The biographical literature on Muhammad written by Muslims and non- Muslims is vast and, not surprisingly, of uneven quality. For the purpose of this essay I refer to three relatively recent books that cover much of what I may only touch upon here. In no order of preference, the first is Clinton Bennett's *In Search of Muhammad* (1998); the second is Tarif Khalidi's *Images of Muhammad: Narratives of the Prophet in Islam Across the Centuries* (2009); and the third is *The Quest for the Historical Muhammad* (2000), edited and translated by Ibn Warraq.

Bennett's study is an effort by a Christian scholar to sift through the literature on Muhammad, taking into account the writings by Muslims and non-Muslims, and through a multi-disciplinary approach that draws upon the methods of critical studies in literature, history, theology and anthropology seek an understanding of Muhammad that is respectful of Muslims without compromising objectivity. This is an admirable effort in achieving, as Bennett describes, "an understanding of what Muhammad means to those for whom he is Prophet, and of what he might, can or does mean for those for whom he is not a Prophet."[3] Khalidi's remarkable book is a compilation of the various images constructed by Muslims through the centuries in their writings in reverence of Muhammad to celebrate, edify, and instruct people about the greatness of their Prophet, and then in the modern age to defend the Prophet from the hostile writings of opponents and critics of Islam. Khalidi's book recalls an earlier study, *And Muhammad Is His Messenger: The Veneration of the Prophet in Islamic Piety* (1987), by Annemarie Schimmel. But Khalidi also refers to the writings of those Muslims in modern times who were influenced by the scientific method and sought, in an attempt to humanize or rescue the Prophet from the midst of superstition and myth-making, "the radical pruning of Muhammad's image from generations of credulity, charlatanry, and prejudice."[4] Ibn Warraq is an ex-Muslim, someone who renounced Islam and acquired considerable reputation in the West as a knowledgeable and formidable opponent of Islam and its Prophet with his first book *Why I Am Not A Muslim* (1995), followed by a number of edited anthologies of critical studies by scholars of Islam on Muhammad and the Qur'an. I will conclude this chapter with my own thoughts on how Muhammad might be viewed in history from a comparative perspective.

The earliest biographical writing about Muhammad available, indeed the first, is from the eighth century, over a hundred years after his demise. Biographical writings are known as *sira*, and *sira* with a capital *S*, as Khalidi reminds us, refers to the biography of Muhammad. *Sira* is the external or outwardly observable narrative of the Prophet's life and career; the details of his conduct reflecting the internal dimension of a life that came to be revered as exemplary by his followers is known as the *sunna*. The *sunna* was collected, organized, given a formal structure, and standardized as *hadīth* or the "traditions" of the Prophet. The collections of the *sunna* begun in the mid-ninth century were systematized and made into the companion of the Qur'an as *hadīth*, and which then formally prescribed the normative standard of ethical/legal conduct for Muslim religious life (faith, prayer, fasting, pilgrimage, charity) patterned after that of the Prophet. *Sira* or the biographical writings about Muhammad remained a sort of independent activity on the part of scholars to which Muslims referred to in order to gain a wider understanding of their Prophet's life as a leader and a statesman engaged in worldly affairs even as he was a Messenger of God (*Rasul Allah*).

The oldest *Sira* is that of Ibn Ishaq (c. 704-767), and it has been the source of all subsequent biographical writings, such as that of al-Tabari (d. 923). The original version of Ibn Ishaq's biography of Muhammad is lost, and what is available is through the redaction of Ibn Hisham (d. 833), which Alfred Guillaume made available through his English rendition, *The Life of Muhammad: A Translation of Ishaq's Sirat Rasul Allah* (1955). Ibn Ishaq set the pattern for subsequent biographers, and any modern biographer of the Prophet claiming his or her work is based on the earliest sources, as Martin Lings does in writing the biography *Muhammad: his life based on the earliest sources* (1983), is going only as far back to Ibn Ishaq. And herein lies the problem. Ibn Ishaq wrote before al-Bukhari and others in the ninth century, more than a century after him, arranged the method or systematization of *hadith*-collection that became the accepted practice of the traditionalist authorities among Muslim scholars of religion. Ibn Ishaq's biography was based on oral reports provided by a chain of transmitters, and the veracity of these oral reports or transmitters he could not authenticate. But Ibn Ishaq was not alone in basing his biography on oral reports. The other three earliest biographers of the Prophet did likewise: Ibn Sa'd (d. 845), al-Baladhuri (d. 892), and al-Tabari. As Khalidi writes,

> Theirs is a *Sira* of primitive devotion, a *Sira* that stands so much in awe of its subject that it gathers in its net all the reports that fall into it, paying little or no heed to their consistency. The guiding principle is inclusion rather than exclusion, and if there are stories or anecdotes about the Prophet that may offend the sensibilities of Muslims, the idea is that it is better for them to remain where they are than be excised because of any pretensions to piety.[5]

It was left to later generations of biographers to strive for consistency in their narratives, to provide normative framework and rules by which the available reports on the life and career of the Prophet were assembled and narrated, and what were considered blemishes in earlier works removed.

The spread of Islam and the making of an Arab-Muslim empire created a market for the *Sira* of the Prophet. As biographies were prepared to meet the demand and the taste of readers, the constructed images of Muhammad became increasingly distant from what little was known of the core details of his life, especially his years spent in Mecca from childhood to his flight to Medina. This core story, as Khalidi writes, could be confined to one paragraph. According to Khalidi,

> Muhammad, son of 'Abdullah son of 'Abd al-Muttalib, was born in Mecca around the year 570 A.D. He began to receive revelations around the year 610 A.D. and shortly thereafter started to preach the faith. During his early years as a preacher he seems to have achieved only a limited success in his hometown, and he had even less success in winning over converts from outside Mecca. The turning point in his career came in the year 622 A.D., when he abandoned Mecca for Medina, a town where he had established a small base of converts who were ready to protect him. This move to Medina (*hijra*) was later adopted by Muslims to mark the first year of the Muslim, or *Hijri*, calendar. From Medina Muhammad organized and often led a series of expeditions whose aim was ultimately to conquer Mecca, "God's sacred precinct," and thereafter spread the religion of Islam inside and outside Arabia. Mecca fell in 630, another landmark year. His followers increased rapidly throughout his years in Medina. The Prophet himself died in Medina in 632.[6]

This core narrative or the bare outline of a life was like a shadow filled out in details, layer upon layer, by Muhammad's followers beginning with Ibn Ishaq till the shadow disappeared behind the montage of images drawn of him to assure Muslims their Prophet was as great as, if not greater than, prophets of the past mentioned in the sacred books of Jews and Christians.

Let us consider the following. By the time Ibn Ishaq completed his *Sira* at some time in the mid-eight century, the desert Arabs united under the banner of Islam had come to rule a vast empire. Within two decades of Muhammad's demise his followers defeated the rulers of the Byzantine Empire in the area of the eastern Mediterranean, conquered Damascus, Jerusalem, and Alexandria, vanquished the Persian Emperor Yazdagird III, seized his capital Ctesiphon, and rapidly conquered his empire on the eastern shores of the Persian Gulf. By the time Ibn Ishaq reached his mature years a century since Muhammad's demise, the Arab-Muslim empire under the Ummayad rulers in Damascus stretched from the plains of the Iberian peninsula or al-Andalus (Spain) in southern Europe across North Africa into Egypt, Syria, the Fertile Crescent, and across the deserts of Persia to the banks of Syr Darya in Central Asia on the western fringes of China and south into the western provinces of India. The speed with which the Arab armies completed this conquest was unprecedented. Over this vast sea of peoples of different ethnicity and culture Arab imperial power was established while Jews, Christians, Zoroastrians, Buddhists, polytheists, and pagans under different circumstances embraced the religion of Arabs, the first followers of Muhammad. In the ranks of these newly converted Muslims whose first language was not Arabic there was demand and, hence, market for biographical details of the Prophet. Ibn Ishaq's biography of Muhammad as such would have been in demand, and Ibn Hisham's redacted edition of Ibn Ishaq's original text circulated widely to meet this growing demand. Other biographies were compiled in the next few centuries after Ibn Ishaq, as Khalidi points out, in which the life of the Prophet was set forth as "canonical, moral, exclusivist, and rationalizing" and Muhammad's "superhuman qualities—his pre-eternity, miraculous powers, and sinlessness" were asserted to fortify the faith of his followers.[7]

The speed with which the Arab-Muslim empire emerged and Islam as a new religion spread outpaced the collection, preparation and formalization of the canonical texts of Islam—the Qur'an and the *hadīth*—and the codification of Islamic law as *Shariah*. These latter acts occurred under the imperial gaze of the rulers, which provided legitimacy to their authority by binding themselves to the requirements prescribed by religion just as Byzantine and Persian rulers did within the frameworks of their respective religions. During this period from the eighth to the tenth century, subsequently described as the Classical Age of Islam, the culture of the Islamic civilization in its fundamentals in terms of religion and law was authoritatively settled. This civilization emerged in contest with the Eastern Roman or Byzantine Empire, and acquired by conquest a vast possession of Eastern Christianity with the Holy Land and ancient cities of historical importance and religious significance to Christians and Jews. The Islamic civilization became the rival, or the *Other*, of Europe as the Christian civilization. And since the central iconic figure of the Christian civilization was Jesus, it meant Muhammad could be no less of an iconic figure for the Islamic civilization. The rivalry and war between Christians and Muslims became transmuted into the war between the Cross and the Crescent, Christianity and Islam, and this hostility between Christians and Muslims ironically implicated Jesus and Muhammad as rivals, if not mortal foes, while their followers viewed their history as outward manifestations of their respective divinely ordained missions on earth.

The rivalry between Christianity and Islam had its effect on the biographical writings of Muhammad by both Muslims and Christians. The dispute about Jesus among Christian sects was settled several centuries before the birth of Muhammad. The Nicene Creed adopted by the Church in 325 A.D. defined for all Christians the true nature of Jesus as "the only-begotten Son of God." Jesus was, therefore, unique and incomparable by the very substance of his nature as the Church declared. Jesus became for Christians the standard by which every founder of a religion or individual preaching in God's name was judged and found inadequate in comparison. And, consequently, anyone who claimed after Jesus to be a prophet, as Muhammad did, could only be someone who was deceitful or an imposter. Muhammad came to be viewed by Christians as an imposter from the very outset of the venture of Islam. His life, narrated by Muslims, was considered by Christians a testimony of the falsehood he preached, and his personal conduct as confirmation of someone committed to deceit, to violence, to sensuality, and engaged in treachery and war to advance his career.

In rejecting Jesus of the Church and Christianity, as the Qur'an does, Islam diminished Jesus in the eyes of Christians. It did not matter that the "Muslim" Jesus, or Jesus of the Qur'an, was a highly venerated and revered prophet gifted with miraculous powers right from his cradle and that his birth to a woman, Mary, untouched by any man was a miracle. But though for Muslims Jesus was a beloved prophet of God, Muhammad could not be seen by his followers being in any way less than what the Qur'an says about Jesus, son of Mary. A portrait of Muhammad as equal to Jesus—or even greater than Jesus for reasons of the worldly success he had in establishing Islam during his lifetime among pagan Arabs—was provided by Muslim biographers of the Prophet.

A Christian Europe threatened by the armies of Islam responded with polemics that vilified Muhammad and his religion. Muslim narratives about Muhammad, in contrast, as the "seal of the prophets" described him in superlatives and obscured the Qur'anic description of him as the simple "warner" or "messenger" preaching against the worshipping of idols or the "witness" affirming the primordial message "there is no deity but Allah" (in the manner of prophets mentioned in the sacred books of Jews and Christians).

From about 1700 Europe came to gradually supersede the Islamic civilization, and by the mid-nineteenth century Europe's power extended across Muslim lands in Africa and Asia. A more confident Europe had less need of strident polemics against Islam and Muhammad, and a more pressing need to understand this "Other" civilization on its own term. The new scientific method of critical inquiry was turned upon Islam, the Qur'an, and its Prophet. The result showed internal inconsistencies in the sacred and canonical literature of Islam and the Prophet. This was not surprising, as similar study of Christianity and its sacred texts had also revealed historical inconsistencies.

The Muslim response to modern inquiry came in the form of apologetic literature. Two writers of Indian birth—Syed Ameer Ali (1849-1928) and Muhammad Iqbal (1877-1938)—are worth mentioning, and Khalidi writes about them in some detail. Ali's book, *The Spirit of Islam: A History of the Evolution and Ideals of Islam with a Life of the Prophet*, first published in 1891, was a spirited defence of the Prophet's nobility in origin and conduct. In a language of great eloquence that was a reminder of the powerful and emotive diction of Thomas Carlyle whose writing on the Prophet was most likely familiar to the author, Ali sought to turn the hostility of the western critics of Muhammad and Islam against them. According to Khalidi, Ali illustrated "how Muhammad's mission can be proven to be more rational and pragmatic, thus more progressive, than that of all other prophets".[8] Iqbal studied philosophy in Germany, and wrote poetry in Urdu and Persian. His lectures to a Muslim audience in Hyderabad, India, were later collected and published in 1930 as *The Reconstruction of Religious Thought in Islam*. Iqbal's lectures were not a biographical study of the Prophet; he spoke, instead, of the renewal of Islam as faith, culture, and civilization consistent with the requirements of the modern age and in harmony with modern science and philosophy.

But modern critical historiography, as Ibn Warraq contends, pointing to the writings of European scholars on Islam such as those of William Muir, Henri Lammens, Ignaz Goldziher, Joseph Schacht and others in recent years, has severely undermined Muslim writings from earliest times about Muhammad. These scholars, according to Ibn Warraq, exposed the weaknesses or fabrications in the writings about the Prophet by the earliest

Muslim historians. But these problems were not new. Ibn Khaldun (1332-1406), born in Tunis, North Africa, and considered by many the greatest philosopher-historian of Islam, discussed these problems in some detail in his major work on historiography known as the *Muqadimmah*.

Ibn Khaldun opened his introduction to the *Muqaddimah*—"An Introduction to History", which is the first part of his multivolume universal *History* (*Kitab al-`Ibar*)—stating, "Historians, Qur'an commentators and leading transmitters have committed frequent errors in the stories and events they reported."[9] He further remarked, "Untruth naturally afflicts historical information. There are various reasons that make this unavoidable."[10] Ibn Khaldun listed seven reasons for errors and untruths found in historical writings, and among them the sixth was "people as a rule approach great and high-ranking persons with praise and encomiums. They embellish conditions and spread their fame."[11] Hence, when it came to historical writings about rulers the common source of errors and untruths was in partisanship, and the urge to embellish the records with encomiums; such errors and untruths, embellishments and encomiums, were predictable problems readily found in the writings of Muslim historians when the subject was the life of the Prophet.

It was similar when it came to the question of authenticity of reports about the Prophet based on a chain of witnesses. Muslims consider Ismail al-Bukhari's collection of *hadīth*—the *Sahīh al-Bukhari*—authoritative. In the course of his work over many years al-Bukhari (810-70), however, set aside as doubtful nearly ninety per cent of some 600,000 reports he collected about the conduct of the Prophet. Similarly, Abu Daud (817-88) rejected some 495,200 reports of the 500,000 he collected as weak or doubtful.[12] Hence, non-Muslim scholars, such as Muir, and Muslim apostates, such as Ibn Warraq, rightly ask if so much of what were considered authoritative reports about the Prophet were set aside as doubtful then how can the rest be accepted as true. But this problem of inconsistencies that might be noted in any religious tradition and is for critics of religions ground for scepticism is ultimately irresolvable, since the subject—the biographical details of the founder of a religion, whether it is Islam, Christianity, Judaism, or Sikhism and Mormonism—is inseparable from the totality of what people of faith accepts as the sacred mystery of their religious belief.

A new approach, under pressure of modern historiography, emerged among some Muslim biographers of Muhammad. The Iraqi poet and literary scholar Ma'ruf al-Rusafi (1875-1945) advanced the radical view, according to Khalidi, that if we wish "to learn about Muhammad as he really was, we have only two safe resorts: the Qur'an—regarded as an accurate historical source—and reason. All other narratives must be subjected to these two criteria before we can accept them."[13] Ali Dashti (1896-1982), a literary scholar, novelist and Iranian senator also took to writing the Prophet's biography. Dashti's *Twenty Three Years* was first published anonymously in Beirut sometime no later than 1974, since writings critical of religion and politics were banned in the last years of the Shah's monarchy in Iran. Dashti went further than al-Rusafi's view in insisting reason must be the primary basis of evaluating and explaining Muhammad's life and career. He questioned the necessity of prophethood and miracles. He suggested the problem of prophethood "be approached from another angle. It should be seen as a sort of mental and spiritual genius peculiar to an extraordinary individual."[14] For Dashti, as it was for al-Rusafi, the Qur'an was evidence of "prophetic eloquence," which empowered Muhammad and brought people to follow him.[15]

A realistic and unapologetic view of Muhammad will be close to the philosophical assessment of the Prophet, as a supremely gifted man as suggested by Iqbal, and to the biographical approach, as illustrated by al Rusafi and Dashti. But first we need to acknowledge the looming presence of Christianity with the iconic image of Jesus on the Cross and what he represents to Christians that dominates the landscape when discussing Islam and Muhammad. The comparison is unavoidable. Here is the image of Jesus as divinity, the "only-begotten Son of God," gentle as the dove who makes no claim to rule in this world. He was unjustly and scandalously condemned for blasphemy in a world where religion was inseparable from politics; he was physically abused and then crucified. The story of Jesus took place inside a mighty empire, that of Rome, under the watchful eyes of the Roman rulers and their Jewish allies and surrogates in Palestine.

The story of Muhammad is strikingly different from that of Jesus on the Cross. Muhammad neither claimed divinity, nor do his followers worship him. Muhammad sought to preach the Word of God in peace, to bring his people to embrace the God of Abraham and to abandon the most primitive form of polytheism, the worship of idols and stones. But faced with the threat of murder he was compelled to flee his native city. He then became deeply enmeshed in the politics of his world far removed from any imperial centre. The world of politics has always been profane, corrupt, and treacherous. It has required cunning to survive, and superior skills in the arts of leadership, diplomacy, and warfare to contend with those in power. Muhammad fought back his enemies and prevailed. He stood out among his people as leader, warrior, and statesman. He destroyed the idols in Mecca, ended idolatry, and by force established monotheism among Arabs that was resisted when he had preached peacefully. There were violence, bloodshed, and war in his life. There were family, wives, children, love, desire, friendship, bereavement, doubts, reversal, persistence, and triumph. In other words, his life was full and open, and a life so lived with such drama as was his could only be one also full of controversy. In the end what mattered most to him was he had been truthfully devoted to the calling of a messenger bearing the Word of God. His success, as tribes from across Arabia came to pledge allegiance to him and embraced the worship of the God of Abraham, was proof that he had remained faithful to the vision that seized him at the beginning of his prophetic career and led him to preach in public what he understood to be a divine message.

Muhammad, on his part, never contested the status of Jesus venerated in the Qur'an. In Martin Lings's biography, based on the earliest sources, the Prophet entered inside the Ka'aba—the sacred precinct built by Abraham and his son, Ismail (Ishmael in the Hebrew Bible), according to tribal legends—on the day Mecca was finally conquered, and then commanded the destruction of all the idols. But he covered the icon of the Virgin Mary with child and a painting reputedly of Abraham that stood there among the Meccan idols by his hand to protect them as the rest were destroyed. This story illuminates Muhammad's respect and affection for Jesus and his mother, and the reverence with which they are described in the Qur'an.[16]

There are very few individuals in history far removed from the living generation who stir impassioned feelings of men and women for good or ill, who are reviled with as much intensity as they are passionately adored, and among them Muhammad is one who stands almost alone for the influence he continues to wield in stirring people's emotions despite the distance in time. Michael Hart, an American scientist and author, ranked Muhammad at the head of his list of the one hundred most influential people in history.[17] In his biography of the Prophet, Maxime Rodinson—a French Marxist historian, atheist and, like Michael Hart, of Jewish origin—wrote,

> Everyone, in fact, has sought in him a reflection of their own doubts and anxieties and those of their time. Everyone has ignored what they have not understood. Everyone has shaped him after their own passions, ideas or fantasies. I do not claim to be immune from this general rule. But even if pure objectivity is unattainable, it would be a sophism to suggest that it was necessary instead to be deliberately partial. We know very little

> for certain about this man whose ideas and actions have shaken the world, but, as with Jesus, we may get, through the unreliable tales and one-sided traditions, a glimpse of something that is the echo of a remarkable personality which astonished the ordinary men who gathered around it.[18]

Muhammad is best likened to the prophets of the Hebrew Bible, ordinary men raised to become instruments of divine providence, as was David, King of the Jews. David was a shepherd raised to kingship, a warrior with the gift of song, a leader who aroused intense feelings among men and women who knew him, a trickster, a seducer, even a murderer, and yet favoured by God. Jonathan Kirsch, in his biography of King David, writes,

> Above all, David illustrates the fundamental truth that the sacred and the profane may find full expression in a single human life, and his biography preserves the earliest evidence of the neurotic double bind that is hardwired into human nature and tugs each of us in different directions at once. Against every effort of Bible-waving moralizers who seek to make us better than we are—or to make us feel bad about the way we are—the biblical account of David is there to acknowledge and even to affirm what men and women really feel and really do.[19]

In the Semitic tradition it is God who acts, and who seeks out the man He wants or favours as His messenger sent to a people as His sign of mercy. God is not indifferent to the fate of humanity. "The Bible speaks not only of man's search for God," wrote Rabbi Abraham Joshua Heschel, "but also of *God's search for man*. 'Thou dost hunt me like a lion,' exclaimed Job."[20] It is God's inscrutable will at play when it comes to creation and revelation. We need to be reminded of Kant's declaration that "Out of the crooked timber of humanity no straight thing was ever made," and yet it is God's preserve of whom He chooses of such timber to be His instrument in the profane world. And so it is God's choosing, irrespective of their flaws, that David, as his name means, was the "beloved," and Muhammad, as his name means, was "worthy of all praise."

Poets understand well instinctively the difference, or distance, between the real and the imagined. T.S. Eliot wrote,

> Between the idea
> And the reality
> Between the motion
> And the act
> Falls the Shadow...[21]

And so it is only of the "shadow" behind all the images of the Prophet constructed across the centuries that we can write of him as the "historical Muhammad." The shadow is the bare outline of his life that we know with some certitude. This bare outline of a shadow belongs to the man, in Rodinson's summation of the Prophet's life, who was "like other men, subject to the same weaknesses and sharing the same powers, Muhammad ibn `Abdallah of the tribe of Quraysh, our brother."[22] In time the shadow became the longing of the heart for the loved one, or the imagined presence of the selfless companion who comforted in an unforgiving world; and into that shadow was poured the tears of people mocked, betrayed, beaten by the powerful in the hope there would eventually be mercy and justice granted to them by their Lord on the "day of reckoning." The rest of the constructed image is how others have seen the Prophet of Islam, and it says as much about them as they venerate him or revile him as it purportedly does about the man some fourteen centuries removed from us.

III.

On the Historical Qur'an

We have sent it down as an Arabic Koran; haply you will understand.

The Qur'an, 12:2.

Thou receivest the Koran from One All-Wise, All-Knowing.

The Qur'an, 27:6.

Nay, but it is a glorious Koran, in a guarded tablet.

The Qur'an, 85:21.

Any query about the historical Qur'an unavoidably implies there is a *non*-historical or *a*-historical Qur'an. Or there is the Qur'an Muslims take as their sacred text and its meaning for them is *extra*-historical. Then there is the Qur'an as a text, a document with history, that like any document may be examined objectively in terms of its origin, preparation, assembly, textual consistency and meaning. And if there are two or more of such texts found, then one looks for variance, interpolations, redaction and other indications that might confirm or alter the authenticity of the text in question. Modern textual criticism and hermeneutics of the Qur'an as a text with history run counter to the views held by the Muslim orthodoxy. Qur'anic exegesis is not lacking among Muslims, though Muslim scholarship, unlike that of non-Muslims, is confined by the traditional formula that the Qur'an is the Word of God revealed to Muhammad.

Any discussion on what is the historical Quran, as it is with the historical Muhammad, is fraught with the peril of, at a minimum, inflicting discomfort on the religious sensibility of Muslims. And yet, I believe, questions about the historical Qur'an are deserving of serious consideration and response. The response of a Muslim might not be convincing to non-Muslim scholars and critics. But a Muslim response would be that of an individual examining the fundamentals of his faith and this would be indicative there are Muslims, however small in numbers, not unwilling to question their orthodox belief. Indeed Muslims, or at least some Muslims, have struggled how best to read the Quran, to interpret it, to reconcile their faith in revelation with reason. And reason would demand of a thinking Muslim to consider the Qur'an objectively while cognizant of the fact that faith is not entirely contained by *reason*, since the "last step that reason takes," as Blaise Pascal noted, "is to recognize that there is an infinity of things beyond it; it is but weak if it does not succeed in recognizing that."[1]

Michael Cook has written, "When we ask how God's speech came to be collected in the form in which we now read it, we leave theology firmly behind us and re-enter the world of history."[2] It is accepted by most historians of Islam that following Muhammad's demise in 632 his followers began collecting all available records of revelation dictated to his scribes and in the possession of individuals who were with him, put them in some order, and prepared one authoritative edition for the Muslim community as it began to grow and spread. What came out of this collective effort spread over nearly two decades was the text of the Qur'an made available to Muslims under the authority of the "rightly-guided" Caliph Uthman, the third caliph or temporal successor of the Prophet. This is the authoritative version of the Qur'an, and this text is taken by Muslims to be the Word of God. According to Cook,

> The book as a whole thus consists always and everywhere of the same 6,200-odd verses in the same order (the exact number depends on the placing of the divisions between the verses, not on the text itself). This striking *invariant* text is known as the 'Uthmanic codex, since according to the standard account it was established on the initiative of the Caliph 'Uthman (ruled 644-

> 56), at some time around 650. (The vagueness of the date arises from the fact that the event seems to have had no place in the early Arabic annalistic tradition.) All the Korans which we possess today represent this recension, though as will be seen, this may not be true of all surviving fragments of the Koranic text.[3]

Here then is the main contention of non-Muslim scholars and critics, as we note in Cook's words, that though the available text referred to as the 'Uthmanic codex is found to be invariant on the whole, there have been fragments found which do not quite fit with this text. The findings of these fragments, and manuscripts in whole or in part of what might well be texts of the Qur'an, lead to questions about textual editing and/or interpolation, and interpretations of the Qur'an that became standard or authorized reading of it.

The discovery in 1972 of very old manuscripts—damaged over the centuries by rain, dampness, rats and insects—inside the Great Mosque of Sana'a, Yemen, renewed the debate over the historical Qur'an. This debate is about whether the collection of the totality of the revelation recorded in written form, verified by those who had committed the revelation to memory, and compiled into a single authoritative text called *mushaf* and referred to by Cook as the 'Uthmanic codex should be accepted as definitive, or if the discovery in Sana'a of old parchments suggests there were other possible arrangements of the *mushaf* different from the compilation we possess. There is also the unresolved issue of how many copies or *mushaf*s were prepared under the directive of 'Uthman and sent to the various garrison towns of the expanding Arab-Muslim empire. Cook writes,

> Once the work was completed, 'Uthman returned the leaves to Hafsa [daughter of Umar, the second Caliph following Abu Bakr, and a widow of the Prophet]. A parallel version of the same narrative tells us that he then sent out a copy of the new text to each of the provinces, and ordered all others to be destroyed.

> One thing this particular account fails to tell us is which provinces received copies. Dani states that they were sent to Kufa, Basra, and Damascus, while one remained in Medina; he adds that a less reliable tradition extends the list to Mecca, Yemen, and Bahrayn.[4]

It is worth noting here that two of the five or six copies Cook mentions are respectively in the possession of the Topkapi Palace Museum in Istanbul, Turkey, and the Tashkent Museum of History in Uzbekistan, and both copies are on display for public viewing.

The Sana'a discovery remains locked, and its findings are unavailable. The cover story "What Is the Koran?" by Toby Lester for the January 1999 issue of *The Atlantic Monthly* focused on the Sana'a discovery and its relevance. Lester wrote,

> The mainly secular effort to reinterpret the Koran—in part based on textual evidence such as that provided by the Yemeni fragments—is disturbing and offensive to many Muslims, just as attempts to reinterpret the Bible and the life of Jesus are disturbing and offensive to many conservative Christians. Nevertheless, there are scholars, Muslims among them, who feel that such an effort, which amounts essentially to placing the Koran in history, will provide fuel for an Islamic revival of sorts—a reappropriation of tradition, a going forward by looking back. Thus far confined to scholarly argument, this sort of thinking can be nonetheless very powerful and—as the histories of the Renaissance and the Reformation demonstrate—can lead to major social change. The Koran, after all, is currently the world's most ideologically influential text.[5]

While we await to learn what the Sana'a discovery will reveal, Andrew Higgins reported in 2008 in the *Wall Street Journal* that a "unique photo archive of ancient manuscripts of the Quran" consisting of 450 rolls of film assembled before the war and believed lost, as a result of bombings on April 24, 1944 that destroyed the Bavarian Academy of Science, has been found safe and undamaged.[6] The study of this photo archive of ancient manuscripts and its findings are also unavailable. But Gerd-R.

Puin, a specialist in Arabic calligraphy and Qur'anic palaeography, was sent by the German government to assist in the restoration project of the Sana'a manuscripts. The only other person, according to Toby Lester, granted permission to examine the Yemeni fragments was Puin's colleague, H.-C. Graf von Bothmer, an Islamic art historian at Saarland University, Saarbrucken. Higgins quoted Puin commenting on this discovery of the photo archive that the Qur'an "didn't just fall from heaven." Puin has written,

> It is true, unfortunately, that the (scriptural) variants are hardly helpful for a better understanding of much of the text which is still far from being as *mubin* ("clear") as the Qur'an claims to be! Thus, even if a complete collection of variants could be achieved, it will probably not lead to a breakthrough in Qur'anic studies. Certainly, though, it will help to reveal the stages of Qur'anic (and Arabic) orthography.[7]

Apart from poring over the textual variants found in fragmentary evidences or parchment manuscripts, as discovered in Yemen and the yet to be disclosed study of the photo archive once held in the Bavarian Academy of Science, the modern hermeneutic study of the Qur'an runs the risk of undermining the traditional or orthodox commentaries of eminent Muslim scholars from the classical period in Islamic history. Though the Qur'an is in the language of the Arabs, the Qur'anic Arabic requires special training to comprehend the scripture. This means the vast majority of Muslims, including Arabs, need commentaries to assist them in understanding the Qur'an. According to Ibn Warraq, a modern non-Muslim or ex-Muslim scholar and critic of Islam:

> The Muslim tradition has woven a fantastic spiderweb around its holy scripture from which even modern scholarship has not managed to disentangle itself. For all Muslims, much of the Koran remains incomprehensible without the commentaries; indeed, that is the very reason there are so many Muslim

> commentaries. As Leemhuis put it, "...The more of the Qur'an that became obscure in the course of time, the more it became provided with an explanation." One would hardly need them if the Koran were truly mubeen, "clear." But...despite all the thousands of pages devoted to clarifying the text, the Koran still remains incomprehensible, even for those Western scholars who accept the traditional, specially chronological Muslim framework of the Koran.
>
> Muslim Koranic exegesis of such influential scholars as Tabari tended to be *tafsir bi'l-ma'thur* (interpretation following tradition), rather than *tafsir bi'l-ra'y* (interpretation by personal opinion). Tabari's great work, *Jami' al-bayan 'an taw' il ay al-Qur'an*, is full of exegetical *hadiths*, where the Prophet gives his explanation of various obscure verses. Similarly, Ibn Kathir advises that if we are unable to elucidate some passage, then one must examine the prophetic *sunna*, and if that fails, then one must have resort to the sayings of the companions of Muhammad.
>
> However, if we accept the negative conclusions of Goldziher, Schacht, Wansbrough, Crone, and Cook about the authenticity of *hadiths* in general, then we must be equally skeptical of the *hadiths* concerning exegesis of the Koran. In other words, we cannot separate discussions of the compilation and meaning of the Koran from the questions about the authenticity of *hadith* and the *sirah*, the life of Muhammad.[8]

This then is the sum total of the problem for critics of Islam and the Qur'an. Apart from what might well be the controversy arising from the examination of fragments of ancient manuscripts of the Qur'an, there remains the accompanying controversy over how to decode the text contextually while setting aside traditional commentaries as unsatisfactory or misleading.

Religion is inseparable from civilization. As the French historian, Fernand Braudel, observed, "religion is the strongest feature of civilizations, at the heart of both their present and their past."[9] In premodern history the higher function of religion was providing legitimacy to power, and those holding power shaped religion, laid down what was authoritative, punished those who dissented and protected the scripture from those who read it differently.

The speed with which the Prophet's generation established an empire did not provide for the space within which the fundamentals of Islam—its scripture and the life of its founder as the model for normative conduct of his followers—could be arranged at some distance from those holding power. The wars of apostasy breaking out on the death of the Prophet and waged by Abu Bakr, the first Caliph, laid the template of the Islamic empire. The well-known *ayat* or verse of the Qur'an reads "No compulsion is there in religion," (2:256). Abu Bakr determined, however, to crush all rebellion among the desert Arabs as apostasy when they refused to pledge loyalty to him. This heavy-handed use of force made a travesty of the Qur'anic injunction that there is no compulsion in religion. Muslims might argue about whether Abu Bakr was right or not, or whether the situation he found with tribes unwilling to accept him as their leader was analogous to the opposition the Prophet confronted in establishing Islam. But the template was set, precedent established, and religious disagreements could be deemed treason. The schismatic wars over succession following the killing of 'Uthman culminated in the murder of Ali, the fourth Caliph, in 661 and the destruction of the Prophet's family at Karbala in 680 when Hussein—Muhammad's grandson by his daughter Fatimah married to Ali—was hacked to death by the opposing army of Yazid ibn Mu'awiyah. These religious political quarrels irrevocably divided Muslims into the two main sects, the majority Sunni and the minority Shi'ite, and influenced the subsequent history of Islam and Muslims. It was in the context of this history, or this history looming in the background, that the compilation of the Qur'an, the writing of the Prophet's early biographies and the collection of his traditions in the making of *hadīth* occurred. And this history was only too recent when the four Sunni schools of law (Hanafi, Maliki, Shafi and Hanbali) and the Shi'ite school (Ja'afari) were founded.

Any modern Muslim scholar has to consider, to be credible, how this early Islamic history has shaped subsequent narrative and understanding of his faith. This early history of Islam is burdened with sectarian controversy, and modern historiography and hermeneutics compound the controversy. Yet there are Muslim scholars who have not flinched in the face of controversy or worse to advance a richer understanding of their religious inheritance. But before I make reference to them here is a perspective of a formidable historian and critic of Islam, even though he was a friend of Muslims and deeply respectful of their faith and culture.

It is not sufficient to affirm how Muslims accept the Qur'an as the Word of God, according to Wilfred Cantwell Smith (1916-2000), since the far greater majority of people do not. The question Smith posed in his Taylor Lectures at the Yale Divinity School for 1963 was "Is the Qur'an the Word of God?" Smith observed:

> Those who have answered it 'yes' have taken the answer passionately. They have been willing to die for it; and what is perhaps more important, if one remarks that people may be stirred to die for many roseate causes, they have been willing to live for it too, to order their lives in accord with it, day after day, year in, year out, generation after generation, patterning their behaviour and controlling their choices and selecting their goals, and to persist, firmly but quietly—against both opposition and distraction, against both attack and indifference—in taking it seriously.
>
> The other group, whose answer has been 'no', have in one sense shown no corresponding passion or fanfare. Yet their persistence has been hardly less steady; and the seriousness of their rejection, not really less. Their conviction has been just as firmly held that the answer is not only 'no', but is obviously 'no'—so obviously 'no' that the matter is not worth bothering about. The West's very indifference to the question is a measure of the profundity of its assurance. Westerners allowed centuries to pass without going around busily asking themselves whether the Quran is the word of God, not because they did not have the

> time or were unconcerned, not because they thought that such issues did not matter (what could matter more?), but because at heart they took for granted that they knew very well what the answer was.
>
> The question, then, is not a minor one. Nor are the groups that have answered it this way or that. It is no small band of eccentrics that holds this book to be God's word; nor is the idea a passing fashion among some volatile crowd. Those who have held it are to be numbered in the many hundreds of millions. And as we have already remarked, it has continued to be held over wide parts of the world for century after changing century. Civilizations are not easy to construct, or to sustain; yet great civilizations have been raised on the basis of this conviction. Major cultures have sprung from it, winning the allegiance and inspiring the loyalty and shaping the dreams and eliciting the poetry of ages proud to bow before its manifest grandeur and, to them, limpid truth...
>
> Equally impressive, however, have been those who have said 'no'. They, too, are not negligible. They, too, are to be numbered in the hundreds or thousands of millions. They, too, have constructed great civilizations, have made great cultures dynamic. The outsider distorts his world if he fails to recognize what has been accomplished on earth by those inspired by the positive response. The Muslim distorts *his*, if he fails to appreciate the possibilities evidently open and beckoning to those who say 'no'.[10]

Smith's question—"Is the Qur'an the Word of God?"—went beyond the differences between Muslims and non-Muslims on matters of faith, to how faith is constituted within a community and with what results. When members of any one faith community insist their understanding of *truth* is the *only* correct understanding, then this has less to do with *truth* in and of itself, and instead reflects the group psychology of that faith community.

The Qur'an is a historical document available to anyone; yet it is, as Smith reminded his audience, more than a text to some very large portion of people in the world, and to them, Muslims, it is a sacred text as the Word of God based on the authority of

Muhammad as the Messenger of God. The sacredness of the Qur'an for Muslims is a matter of *belief*, where belief remains *a priori* to reasoning. Belief may be buttressed by reason; but reason is insufficient by itself to confirm faith, since it can neither prove nor disprove belief. Religious *truth* is not simply a subject of academic or scholarly discourse that may be assessed by a logical method for consistency and appeal; its test lies in the *conduct* of believers. An excellence of belief can only be judged by the excellence of conduct; hence a plurality of faiths does not obstruct good conduct, and the Qur'an instructs "excel in good deeds." The matter of whether the Qur'an is, or is not, the Word of God might be set aside since it is a matter of belief; what matters, instead, is to assess, in response to the Word of God, how adequately or inadequately Muslims have contributed to the general welfare of mankind.

Muslim understanding of the Qur'an has varied and has been contentious. An early dispute arose over the question whether the Qur'an was created in time as God addressed Muhammad, or the Qur'an being eternal was uncreated and coeval with God. This dispute had far ranging theological and philosophical implications for at its center were the issue of revelation and reason. Those known as *Mu`tazilîs* or rationalists took the view the Qur'an was created as God's Word revealed to Muhammad. They believed humans were gifted with free will and this made humans responsible and accountable on the day of reckoning. But the *Mu`tazilî* or the rationalist school of thinking was declared heretical by the orthodoxy, especially among the majority Sunni Muslims. The orthodoxy took the Qur'an literally, and insisted only *revelation*, not reason and irrespective of any reasoning Muslims were instructed on what was good and what was forbidden. The orthodox victory over *Mu`tazilîs* brought an end to independent reasoning among Muslims fearful of denunciation as heretics. Islamic orthodoxy became the traditional consensus, and in holding it Muslims—majority Sunni Muslims in particular—

proceeded to build an Islamic civilization until eventually Europeans surpassed it.

In the shadow of the European civilization Muslims began questioning their history. It would invariably place their faith under scrutiny. In Egypt Muhammad 'Abduh (1849-1905), as did his teacher Jamal-ad-din "al Afghani" (1838-97), struggled to find harmony between revelation and reason; and in India Sayyid Ahmed Khan (1817-1898), a contemporary of 'Abduh, struggled similarly to reconcile faith and reason. But traditionalists remained firm despite the efforts of 'Abduh, Khan and like-minded reformist Muslims.

In 1925 Ali 'Abd al-Razik (1888-1966) published *al-Islam wa Usul al-Hukm* ("Islam and the Fundamentals of Authority"). Al-Razik was a student of 'Abduh and his book took Egypt and the Muslim world by storm. He defended the abolition of the Caliphate on religious grounds, and contended Islam was exclusively a spiritual community and not a political doctrine. He wrote,

> The truth is, that the religion of Islam is innocent of this caliphate with which the Muslims are acquainted, and innocent of all that which they have arranged about it, in ways of desire and fear and in the way of might and power.[11]

In India Muhammad Iqbal (1877-1938), a contemporary of al-Razik, questioned orthodoxy, and argued in favour of new thinking consistent with the modern world. In Iqbal's view the Qur'an was about awakening man to his divinely gifted potential. He wrote, "Its main purpose, as I have said before, is to awaken in man the higher consciousness of his relation with God and the universe."[12] Muslim modernists following 'Abduh and Khan, al-Razik and Iqbal, would venture further in the exegesis of the Qur'an believing that God's Word being eternal could not be kept bound by the views of earlier generations of Muslims.

It is an old controversy whether the Qur'an was Muhammad's fabrication or not. The Qur'an states, "Or do they say, 'He has forged it'? Say: 'Then bring you ten suras [verses] the like of it, forged; and call upon whom you are able, apart from God, if you speak truly.'" (11:16). Yet the controversy persists. It is an article of faith for Muslims that the Qur'an is the Word of God. Indeed, before there was a text compiled of the revelation, there was only the Word of God as heard by Muhammad, and it was through Muhammad that the Word was received by others. Fazlur Rahman (1919-88), a Muslim scholar and philosopher of Indo-Pakistani origin, proposed a radical interpretation by pointing out that the pristine Qur'an was Muhammad's divinely inspired speech before the 'Uthmanic codex was compiled. This got him into deep trouble with the orthodoxy and he was forced into exile. Rahman wrote,

> But orthodoxy (indeed, all medieval thought) lacked the necessary intellectual tools to combine in its formulation of the dogma the otherness and verbal character of the Revelation on the one hand, and its intimate connection with the work and the religious personality of the Prophet on the other, i.e. it lacked the intellectual capacity to say both that the Qur'an is entirely the Word of God and, in an ordinary sense, also entirely the word of Muhammad. The Qur'an obviously holds both, for it insists that it has come to the 'heart' of the Prophet, how can it be external to him?[13]

Rahman's answer to the old question was bold, yet carefully formulated. Others, such as Ma'ruf al-Rusafi (1875-1945), Iraqi poet and literary critic and Ali Dashti (1896-1982), Iranian scholar, novelist and senator, were more direct in maintaining the Qur'an is the speech of Muhammad, inspired, eloquent, forceful and seemingly miraculous. If we view the Qur'an as Rahman suggests, or accept the views of al-Rusafi and Dashti, inconsistencies then can be explained in terms of Muhammad's own struggle with the world around him, while he remained seized by the vision of God. This would explain such instances as the controversy surrounding the Satanic verses, references to Muhammad's life in terms of his difficulties in marriages, the incident with Ayesha and the rumours floated that were insulting to him, the incident with the blind man, or his marriage to the divorced spouse of his adopted son, all of which raise the question why should such matters be found in the Qur'an as the Word of God eternally preserved. The orthodoxy holds to the belief that the eternity of the Qur'an meant that God knew ahead of time events in Muhammad's life. The relevant verse of the Qur'an reads, "it is a glorious Koran, in a guarded tablet" (85:21). A modern reading of this verse might well be the Qur'an is eternally preserved in the hearts of men and women, as it was indeed in Muhammad's heart, and generates God-consciousness or devotion in a believer. Muhammad's occasional struggles with temptations or weakness of mind would then be instances of his inner conflict spoken truthfully as found recorded in the Qur'an.

We might imagine how Muhammad likely would have responded if told he was founding a new religion. The Qur'an repeatedly informs Muhammad was a messenger (*rasul*) bearing the primordial message of the Oneness of God. Moreover, the Qur'an reconfirmed for pagan Arabs stories told by Jews and Christians and with which they were familiar. Muhammad's mission was to bring pagan Arabs into the fold of Abraham's monotheism, and this mission was not unlike that of Paul who carried the good news of Jesus into the world of pagan Gentiles.

Some thirty years after the lecture Smith gave at the Yale Divinity School, he returned to thinking about the Qur'an as scripture. Smith wrote that "to understand the Qur'an as scripture one must recognize it as scripture."[14] He insisted when Muslims take the Qur'an as scripture others should also take it as scripture when studying it, and not merely as another text. This was not simply a matter of politeness; it was about how to engage as an outsider with a religious tradition. And a scripture, any scripture, according to Smith, "means, what it in fact means, and has meant, to those for whom it has been meaningful."[15] Smith was a critic of the Enlightenment rationality when it came to religion, and he believed "the modern analytic mode of thinking has itself been inherently oriented away from human wholeness, and creativity, and synthesizing vision."[16] He wrote, "The real meaning of the Qur'an is not any one meaning but is a dynamic process of meanings, in variegated and unending flow."[17] Much earlier Iqbal had written, "The teaching of the Qur'an that life is a process of progressive creation necessitates that each generation, guided but unhampered by the work of its predecessors, should be permitted to solve its own problems."[18] Smith leaned towards post-modern epistemology as the search for meaning in texts instead of being confined by the authoritativeness of texts, and he came to agree with Iqbal.

Iqbal's reading of the Qur'an was also reflective of his understanding as to why Islam as a civilization decayed. He believed Muslims deferred to their past history in an uncritical manner that crippled them intellectually, culturally and politically to confront the challenges facing them in the present. Muslim scholars in recent years have pushed deeper and further in the direction charted by Iqbal and his contemporaries.

There was Mohammed Arkoun (1928-2010), an Algerian who lived and taught in France, for whom "rethinking Islam" meant liberating Qur'anic discourse from the authority of the "Closed Official Corpus" of the Muslim community. Arkoun welcomed western critics' questions and examined the traditional study of the Qur'an in terms of modern historiography, anthropology, sociology and deconstructed the dominant orthodox view that conflated traditional interpretation of the Qur'an with divine revelation. The authority of the past invariably becomes dogmatic and, Arkoun wrote, "dogmas become stakes in the game of politics."[19] In Egypt the non-traditional approach of 'Abduh and al-Razik was pushed further by Hassan Hanafi (b. 1935) and Nasr

Hamid Abu Zaid (1943-2010) at great risks from activists of the Muslim Brotherhood and its allies. Nasr Hamid was declared an apostate and forced into exile in Holland with his wife. He had contended, as a hermeneutist, for distinguishing between Qur'an as God's Word and human understanding of it. He wrote, "God's Word exists in a sphere beyond human knowledge, but we can apply hermeneutical principles to a text that exists in time and place."[20] In other words, while the Qur'an is divine its interpretation can only be human.

There is the Iranian thinker Abdolkarim Soroush (b. 1945), who took leave of Ayatollah Khomeini's regime to pursue his studies in modern philosophy. Soroush has sought to distinguish between "Islam as identity" and "Islam as truth"; the former, he suggests, is a guise for cultural identity and a response to the "crisis of identity," while the later refers to Islam as a repository of truth. He writes,

> [T]he latter can coexist with other truths; the former, however, is, by its very nature, belligerent and bellicose. It is the Islam of war, not the Islam of peace. Two identities would fight each other, while two truths would cooperate.[21]

Nasr Hamid and Soroush read the Qur'an as an open book wherein the colloquy of God is unending. This approach is also found in the work of Farid Esack (b. 1959), a South African scholar of Islam. And such an approach brought Esack to draw upon his "South African Muslim heritage in explaining what the Qur'an means to Muslims."[22] Among women thinkers there was Fatema Mernissi (1940-2015), a Moroccan anthropologist, and her reading of the Qur'an provided a feminist view in a world increasingly aware of itself in term of interdependent cultures. There is a common thread in this growing body of Muslim scholars which ties them together in the contemporary world of change and upheaval, of greater self-awareness among people of all nationalities in various socioeconomic situations, of co-operation and competition. This thread is their commitment to engage in *ijtihād*—the effort invested in independent reasoning—as the tool by which to maintain faith in their religious tradition, to draw spiritual nourishment and guidance from the Qur'an, and to help Muslim societies find their internal equilibrium in order to be at peace with others.

The historical Qur'an is a text that has history in terms of its compilation and how it is read and understood by successive generations of Muslims and non-Muslims. Before the Qur'an was compiled into a text It (the Qur'an) was, however, the Word of God revealed only to Muhammad. What has come down to us through fourteen centuries as a compilation or *mushaf* are scratches on leaves of paper that can never be turned into the sound, the rhythm, the majesty of the Word declaimed by the Prophet to those around him. For if this could be imagined it would be as if someone on reading a text of Enrico Caruso's favourite aria could hear the tenor of his great voice soaring above an audience held in rapture by his incomparable performance. The historical Qur'an is a text distinct from the revelation a Muslim recites, commits to memory, and which he believes draws him near by imitating Muhammad, the Prophet of Islam, to the Lord of the Universe and Master of the Day of Reckoning whose mercy he seeks.

IV.

The Qur'an Problem

'Peace!'—such is the greeting, from a Lord All-Compassionate.
The Qur'an, 36:58.

It is He who sent down upon thee the Book, wherein are verses clear that are the Essence of the Book, and others ambiguous.
The Qur'an, 3:5.

"There are many faces of Islam," or "there are many Islam," are not original observations. But they have been obscured by the immensity of the general upheaval inside the Muslim world over the past half-century. This upheaval continues to take a heavy toll on Muslims and non-Muslim minorities, and in our contemporary world of round-the-clock media and digital technology of instant global communications in words and pictures this upheaval gets amplified with insufficient reference to history. The result is Muslim fanatics driven by their lust for blood and power have succeeded in defining Islam in their image.

The global Muslim population in 2015 was in excess of 1.5 billion, which amounted to around one-fifth, compared to Christians at nearly one-third, of the world population. This number is rapidly increasing and in percentage term—according to the figures of the Pew Research Center—by the year 2050 Muslims estimated at 2.8 billion will approximately equal Christians estimated at 2.9 billion, and in the next half of the twenty-first century Muslims will exceed the global Christian population.[1] These numbers tell only part of the story of Islam and Muslims in our world. The more significant part of the story is that while the Muslim world is ethnically and culturally diverse, it is located within the boundaries of what was until lately described as the "third world" burdened with the relative problems of poverty, population explosion, resource depletion, and socioeconomic backwardness when compared with the rich and highly advanced technological societies of Europe, North America, East Asia (Japan, South Korea, Taiwan), Australia and New Zealand, including Israel.

The largest number of Muslims, or about four-fifth of the global Muslim population, resides outside of the Middle East complex in the Asia-Pacific region. Of this number most Muslims are of South Asian origin, and the three largest Muslim countries following Indonesia are India, Pakistan, and Bangladesh. The next largest Muslim country by population is Nigeria followed by Egypt, an Arab state. This demographic snapshot of the Muslim world illustrates the reality that the non-Arab Muslim population vastly outnumbers Muslims of Arab ethnicity.

Islam is a world religion with a global presence, as is Christianity and Buddhism. But for different reasons among Muslims and non-Muslims alike there is a fixation on Arabs within Islam. Among non-Arab Muslims this fixation is tied to the notion that since Muhammad was an Arab by birth and the Qur'an was revealed in Arabic, Arabs are viewed as the better exponents and representatives of Islam than non-Arab Muslims; and among non-Muslims Islam has been conflated with Arabs from its beginning, while in modern times oil, petrodollars, and the Arab-Israeli conflict have provided Arabs an undeserving or exaggerated importance in how Islam gets defined and understood by non-Muslims.

The Middle East contains less than a fifth of the total global Muslim population, yet it is the central region of the world of Islam and the main driver of the contemporary upheaval. The effects of this upheaval—"the crisis of Islam" in Bernard Lewis's description—have been felt beyond the region. The terrorist attacks of September 11, 2001 in New York City and Washington, followed by terrorist attacks in Madrid, London, Paris, Brussels,

Berlin, and elsewhere have drawn the West into this upheaval. There is a multiplicity of factors—social, economic, political, demographic, cultural, geological, environmental—that came together in pushing the region into a combustion that eventually should exhaust itself and in its aftermath Muslims, Arabs and non-Arabs (Afghans, Berbers, Iranians, Kurds, Turks) in the Middle East will face the same agonizing set of problems they were convulsed with before the upheaval.

"Modernization," wrote Octavio Paz (1914-1998), the Mexican poet, essayist, diplomat and the 1990 Nobel Prize winner in Literature, "means adoption and adaptation of the civilization of the West, above all its science and technology."[2] The central problem for Muslims yet unresolved is how to embrace modernization as change in the realm of culture, since modernity bearing the stamp of the secularized West has been viewed by great many Muslims as un-Islamic, or anti-Islamic, and feared it will wreck their inherited traditional pre-modern culture.

The anti-monarchical Iranian revolution of 1979, which brought Ayatollah Ruhollah Khomeini (1902-1989), a Shi'a Muslim theologian and jurist, to power was fueled in large part by fear of and hostility against the Shah's program of modernizing a traditional society. Some intellectuals of the Iranian revolution ridiculed modernization as a disease, and they named it mockingly as "Westoxification" or "Weststruck".

The Iranian revolution marked the beginning of the reversal of the previous half-century of effort in modernizing the Middle East following World War I and the dismantling of the Ottoman Empire. This modernizing effort was initiated and vigorously pushed by Mustafa Kemal Atatürk (1881-1938) in the making of Turkey as a secular republic after he abolished the Caliphate based in Istanbul, which represented the main religious-political institution of the majority Sunni Islam founded by the companions of Muhammad after his death. Atatürk set the example for Iran under the Shah (1919-1980), and for post-colonial Arab states such as Egypt under Gamal Abdel Nasser (1918-1970) and Tunisia under Habib Bourguiba (1903-2000).

The traditional reaction against modernization may be explained as opposition to freedom in terms of individual rights, and equality of all in society that would nullify unequal status between Muslims and non-Muslims and between men and women. The Muslim Brotherhood (*Ikhwān al-Muslimīn*) in Egypt joined by other related organizations, such as the Jamaat-i-Islami in South Asia, mobilized the reactionary resistance to modernization under the flag of Islam, and with them medieval theology as political ideology of Islamism was revived and exported across the Muslim world as "authentic Islam." Hasan al-Banna (1906-1949), the founder of the modern *Ikhwān*, and Sayyid Qutb (1906-1966), considered by many observers of contemporary Arab history as "the theoretician par excellence of Islamic resurgence," were both deeply influenced by the politics of the era between the two world wars of the last century. They also became the most determined opponents of modernity and the West by framing their politics in theological terms.

Political Islam, or Islamism, has a long pedigree reaching back to the earliest years of Islam. Its modern proponents, the followers of Hasan al-Banna and Sayyid Qutb, of Khomeini and the Indo-Pakistani Maududi, accordingly insist their practice of Islam as *jihād* or holy war to spread the Shariah (Islamic laws) is authentic, definitive, and any departure from their construct of Islam is heresy. Political Islam, instead, has incited violence among Muslims that has reached beyond the confines of the Middle East in like manner of the early conflicts within Islam beginning in the first century of its history.

At the core of contemporary political Islam is the claim that Islam means *jihād* to establish and secure God's law derived from the Qur'an everywhere by persuasion or by force. Sayyid Qutb made this argument the central pillar of his theology of *jihād*. Since this Qutbian theology was devoted to the revival of Islam it mapped the pathway—the "signposts" or the "milestones"—of how this was to be done.

In *Milestones*—Qutb's most widely distributed work that might be compared to Lenin's *What is to be Done?*—the theorist of *jihād* asserted that the Qur'an, as the sacred text of Islam, instructed Muslims on how to wage *jihād* and establish God's dominance over the world. Islam's revival required, according to Qutb, retrieving what he considered the essential message of the Qur'an—*jihād* (holy war)—and making it the priority once again. Qutb believed that the misreading of the Qur'an had obscured its message of *jihād* and what was required of Muslims in renewing Islam was re-learning the lesson from the first generation of Muslims on how to spread Islam, since that generation was privileged to hear the Qur'an and receive instruction from the Prophet in person.

While Qutbian theology re-introduced Muslims in the second-half of the twentieth century to theologians from the medieval era, especially ibn Taymiyya, it once again brought to the fore-front questions on how to read, interpret, and understand the Qur'an in the context of our modern world. This is, in my view, *the Qur'an problem*: for since "there are many faces of Islam"—(Sunni, Shi'a, Ismaili, Zaydi, Alawi, Ahmadiyya, Wahhabi, Sufi, Ibadi, etc.,)—then there are many different readings of the Qur'an, and the claim of Islamists that Islam is invariant and the meaning of the Qur'an is fixed for all times is spurious and indefensible. It is, in fact, a *lie* perpetrated by Islamists against Muslims in general.

ii.

It is true all scriptures are texts, but not all texts are scriptures. The Torah, the New Testament, and the Qur'an are scriptures as sacred texts of Jews, Christians, and Muslims; but so are the Vedas, the Puranas, the Sutras, and the Avesta the sacred texts of Hinduism, Jainism, Buddhism, and Zoroastrianism. What makes these texts scriptures is the belief invested in them by people that the source of each of these texts is supernatural.

In What *Is Scripture? A Comparative Approach*, Wilfrid Cantwell Smith (1916-2000) suggested, *"scripture is a human activity."* Smith wrote,

> The human involvement is central. We take it as a firm sequel to modern historical awareness that the quality of being scripture is not an attribute of texts. It is a characteristic of the attitude of persons—groups of persons—to what outsiders perceive as texts. It denotes a relation between a people and a text. Yet that too is finally inadequate. As we shall see more fully later, at issue is the relation between a people and the universe, in the light of their perception of a given text.[3]

When Muhammad preached his message in the early seventh century Arabia in the light of the revelation he claimed he had received from the God of Abraham that "there is no god but God," it was rejected not only by the idol worshippers in Mecca, but also by Jews in Medina when he immigrated to that town. Jews had their own scripture, and they were not prepared to accept the revelation Muhammad claimed was God's Word as substitute for, or fulfillment of, what they held to be God's Word according to their scripture.

Several centuries before Muhammad's birth a similar event occurred in and around Jerusalem in which Jesus was at its center. Jews of Palestine (ancient Judea and Samaria) rejected any claim of Jesus, or that of his disciples, that he was the Messiah as promised by God in their scripture. Later when Jesus was presented in the gospels of his close disciples as the Son of God, Jews among whom Jesus was born viewed it as blasphemy. Much later Muhammad, according to the revelation he claimed was God's Word, mocked the notion that God would bear a child and affirmed that Jesus was, instead, of miraculous birth and one of the most esteemed prophets of God.

Scriptures provided identity to people and set them apart from each other by the nature of their worship and their respective history. Scriptures demarcated territorial space within which people arranged the manner of their living, of how they were governed, and who among them rightfully held power directing their affairs in times of peace and war. Scriptural authority legitimated politics and, hence, in pre-modern times politics was in some form or other "theopolitics".[4]

The claims made by any people that their scripture was one of universal appeal, as in the claims of Christians with their New Testament or Muslims with their Qur'an, was belied by the reality that others rejected their claims. The borders that came to be demarcated and defended by people identified by their respective scriptures—for Christians the territories of Christendom, for Muslims *Dār al-Islam* (the House of Islam)—were the limits within which the scriptural authority of one people prevailed and the frontiers where began the rule of another scriptural authority. Whatever the material cause (plunder, territorial expansion, dynastic ambitions) of a particular war between two ruling powers, it became a religious war. Similarly, disputes among people who believed in the authority of the same scripture became sectarian wars, and on the outcome of such disputes hung in balance how the scripture was read and its meaning understood.

The internal sectarian disputes among people and their results have proven to be of immense consequence for the subsequent history of that people. The internal disputes among Christians, spread over a millennium from the conversion of the Roman Emperor Constantine in the early fourth century to the beginnings of the Renaissance era in Italy in the fourteenth century, eventually led to the philosophical and scientific revolutions in the making of modern Europe. For Muslims, on the contrary, internal sectarian disputes culminated about a millennium ago in the homicide of philosophy within the mainstream majority culture of Sunni Islam that became a catastrophe for their subsequent history.

iii.

Before there was the Qur'an put together in written form under Uthman, the third Caliph (644-656), it was the Word recited and memorized that Muhammad claimed he had received from God of Abraham through the agency of the archangel Gabriel (*Jibrīl* in Arabic). It was said of Muhammad, according to the tradition as narrated by his wife Ayesha, that he was the "walking Qur'an."

If Muhammad had not prevailed against the opposition he faced, the history of Arabs would not have taken the direction it took during and after his life. Disputes and conflicts during the twenty-three years in his role as God's messenger (*rasul Allah*) he settled according to, as he claimed, what was revealed to him.

Revelation for Muhammad was a physical encounter with Gabriel. The Qur'an describes the encounter as follows:

> This is naught but a revelation revealed,
> taught him by one terrible power,
> very strong; he stood poised,
> being on the higher horizon,
> then drew near and suspended hung,
> two bows-length away, or nearer,
> then revealed to his servant that he revealed (53: 4-10).[5]

In the modern secular age the idea of revelation belongs to the past. However, the insight offered by Friedrich Schleiermacher (1768-1834), German Biblical scholar and theologian, in *On Religion* remains instructive. Schleiermacher wrote, "What is revelation? Every original and new communication of the Universe to man is a revelation."[6] For Jews, Christians, and Muslims revelation has meant man's encounter with God and of God revealing, or "unveiling", himself to man. These encounters are matter of belief and taken as a testimony of faith. For Jews it was

God's encounter with Moses; for Christians it was God revealed in *flesh* as Jesus; and for Muslims it was the *Spoken Word* of God, the Qur'an, revealed to Muhammad.

There could be no disputation with Muhammad by those around him on what was meant by the Spoken Word revealed to him. He was the messenger of what was revealed and its best exponent. Disputes predictably arose over the meanings of the message revealed to Muhammad after he was no longer around to settle them. At first dispute arose over the question of who among his companions should be his successor as leader or Caliph (in Arabic *khalifa*) of Arabs. This was followed by disputes and wars—the "Ridda wars" or the Wars of Apostasy—when some Arab tribes who had pledged loyalty to Muhammad indicated they did not owe the same to Abu Bakr as the Caliph.

Muhammad had made no claim of founding a new religion, and at his death he had not established an entity that could be described in any real sense as a state. According to M.A. Shaban in *Islamic History: A New Interpretation*,

> In all his activities Muhammad was no innovator and he repeatedly emphasized this point. Even his religion was not new. He insisted that it had always been there and it was no different from that of previous prophets beginning with Abraham... [He] did not establish a state, nor did he unite the Arabs. He took over an existing established regime and modified it, introducing as few changes as possible.[7]

The intensity of early disputes following Muhammad's death renewed the intra-tribal conflicts among Arabs of his generation. There was bloodshed, divisions among the companions of the Prophet, and the Caliphs Umar and Uthman succeeding Abu Bakr were killed. But the surprising successes of Muslims against the armies of the Byzantine and Persian empires brought a new challenge to the fledgling Arab leadership on how to administer lands and peoples that were swiftly conquered, and for which there was neither mandate in the Qur'an, nor instructions left behind by the Prophet of Islam.

It was said of the British Empire that it came about in a fit of absent-mindedness. Arabs of Muhammad's generation acquired an empire without forethought or planning, if not quite absent-mindedly. It came about *opportunistically* and would be hugely consequential in determining what came to be the officially sanctioned culture of traditional Islam. Historical Islam in effect was shaped by the bloody discord over who would succeed Muhammad as the temporal leader of Muslims, and by the weight of empire the earliest generation of Arabs acquired with an astonishing speed. And thus the seeds of political Islam sown by the Caliphs, as immediate successors of the Prophet, grew rapidly to obscure the face of the "other Islam". This "other Islam" was embodied in the example of Abraham presented in the Qur'an as *hanif*, meaning a true believer, someone who turned away from serving idols to worship God who, as the Qur'an repeatedly reminds people, "created heaven and earth."

Both the Persians and the Byzantines after more than half-millennium of mutually destructive warfare waged against each other were exhausted powers when Arabs appeared on their frontiers during the early decades of the seventh century. The disputes among Christians regarding the nature of Jesus as divine had also weakened from within the Byzantine Empire. The church fathers gathered at the first Council of Nicaea in 325 at the behest of Emperor Constantine had worked to end the Christological debate over Jesus's divinity, but three centuries later as Muhammad struggled against the Arabs of the desert the internal conflicts among Christians turned ominous. The "Jesus Wars", in Philip Jenkins description, stretched over several centuries after Nicaea and made the Byzantine Empire vulnerable. When the first Arab armies bearing the flag of Islam poured across the Byzantine frontier in Syria the result was not surprising. According to Jenkins,

> The split within ancient Christianity prepared the way for outside powers who would exploit intra-Christian divisions—first the Persians, and eventually the Muslims. Without that great split, the rise of Islam would have been unthinkable. Without the religious crisis, Islam could not have stormed into political near-vacuum it found in the seventh century, into an empire where most Eastern subjects—Monophysite and Nestorian—rejected their Orthodox/Catholic emperors. So alienated were the Christian dissidents that few were prepared to resist Muslim invaders, who promised (and practiced) tolerance for the diverse Christian sects. In its earliest phases, the new faith offered a clean break from the historic cycle of violence and persecution that had so disfigured late-antique Christianity.[8]

The success of Arab armies made the nascent Arab state rich, as immense wealth poured into the treasury administered by the Caliph. It provided incentive to the tribal elites to settle the internal quarrels that had turned bloody and costly. Following Uthman's murder, Ali ibn Abi Talib, cousin and son-in-law of the Prophet, was acclaimed as the fourth Caliph in 656. But the kinsmen of Uthman led by Mu`awiya, the governor of Syria resident in Damascus, wanted his killers brought to justice and Ali found himself in a difficult situation among disaffected tribal leaders and their supporters.

Ali was known as a man of integrity and courage. He had been close to Muhammad whose favorite daughter, Fatima, was given in marriage to him as a token of the special relationship binding them. Yet there were internal tensions in the Prophet's household as a result of Ayesha's dislike of Ali. Seemingly forgotten misunderstandings from the past bubbled to the surface following Uthman's murder, and there were reports that Ayesha's brother was among the killers of the third Caliph.

In Medina rivalry between the *muhājirun* (the Meccans who found refuge in the city with Muhammad after he fled Mecca) and the *ansār* (the people of the city who had invited the Prophet and accommodated those who came with him) was unsettled. Ali was drawn into the vortex of these quarrels. A conflict ensued, known as the Battle of the Camel, in which Ayesha rode into the melee at the head of Meccans against supporters of Ali in the vicinity of Basra in Iraq. Ali defeated the rebels and sent Ayesha back in safety to Mecca.

But the more serious challenge to Ali came from Mu`awiya in Syria. Mu`awiya refused to recognize Ali as the leader of the faithful (*Amir al Mu'minīn*). Their two armies met in 657 at Siffin near the Euphrates. The battle had barely begun when Mu`awiya's Syrian soldiers raised their spears with sheets of verses from the Qur'an tied on them in an appeal for arbitration. Ali felt compelled to heed the request, but this decision weakened him among his supporters. The discontent spread and eventually Ali was killed in Kufa, Iraq, in 661.

The use of the Qur'an by Mu`awiya to stalemate Ali was an ingenious move by a man known for his cunning. It was also a dramatic display of how the Qur'an could be used, and read, for political purposes and personal gains by a companion of the Prophet in the name of Islam. The Battle of Siffin set the precedent for partisan use of the Qur'an in political disputes, and ever since every Muslim ruler or usurper has raised the Qur'an in justifying his political authority.

Mu`awiya proclaimed himself Caliph in Jerusalem in 660, made Damascus his capital, and founded the Umayyad Caliphate as the first dynasty of Arab rulers that became the norm within historical Islam. Mu`awiya was ironically a son of Abu Sufyan, one of the clan elders in Mecca and a bitter foe of Muhammad. Abu Sufyan had led the campaigns against Muhammad in Medina, and was among the last of the Quraysh chiefs to accept Islam on the day Mecca fell in 630 to the Prophet and his followers. During Mu`awiya's rule (660-680) the expanding Arab-Islamic empire took the form of previous empires that had ruled over the region, and he can be portrayed as an Arab version of the Roman

Emperor Augustus. In mentioning the Umayyad dynasty, Arnold Toynbee in *A Study of History* commented,

> In the conquered provinces of the Roman and Sassanian Empires the alternatives offered were not 'Islam or death' but 'Islam or a super-tax'—a policy traditionally praised for its enlightenment when pursued long afterwards in England by a Laodicean Queen Elizabeth. Nor was this option made invidious for the non-Muslim subjects of the Arab Caliphate under the Umayyad regime, for the Umayyads (with the exception of a single representative of the line, who reigned for only three years) were Laodiceans to a man. In fact the Umayyads were personally crypto-pagans who were indifferent, or even positively hostile, to the propagation of the Islamic faith of which they enjoyed titular leadership.[9]

Mu`awiya lived long enough to arrange for his son, Yazid, to succeed him. When this occurred followers of Ali in Kufa, Iraq, persuaded Hussein, Ali's younger son and the Prophet's grandson, to contest the legitimacy of Yazid's appointment. It ended tragically. Hussein was slain together with the male members of his retinue in an encounter with Yazid's soldiers at Karbala, Iraq, in 680. The martyrdom of Hussein and the dynastic nature of the Umayyad rule turned the internal tribal conflicts among Arabs into permanent sectarian divide within Islam between the majority Sunni (those who accepted the consensus of the community in following the traditions of the Prophet) and the minority Shi'a (the partisans of Ali, or those who accepted the traditions of the Prophet as reported only by Ali and his male descendants). The Qur'an since then has been read, understood, and interpreted differently by Sunni Muslims and Shi'a Muslims.

iv.

The Abbasid revolution of 750 swept the Umayyad dynasty from power, moved the capital from Damascus to Baghdad, and opened a new chapter in Islamic history. There was mingling of Arabs and non-Arabs, primarily Persians, under the new dispensation, which contributed to a burst of cultural outpouring in late antiquity.

A survivor of the massacre of the Umayyad dynasty in Damascus found his way to Spain or *al-Andalus*, and eventually in Cordoba established rule in the name of his family. At the two ends of the Mediterranean two rival Caliphates—the Abbasid in Baghdad and the Umayyad in Cordoba—illuminated the ancient world for a few centuries with patronage of men of letters irrespective of their personal beliefs or origins. It was the high noon of the Islamic civilization.

For five centuries Baghdad and Cordoba were two eminent centers of learning in antiquity. Here the philosophical treasures of ancient Greece were translated into Arabic and studied by the most notable men of their times who sought to reconcile revelation (Qur'an) and reason (philosophy). The discovery of Aristotle sparked intense debates among learned Muslims, Jews, and Christians around the shores of the Mediterranean on questions relating to the existence and proof of God, on creation and the mysteries of nature, and how the rationalism of pagan philosophers, such as Aristotle, could be reconciled with religious belief. Al-Kindi, a ninth century Arab thinker and considered one of the founders of Muslim philosophy, reputedly declared, "It is fitting then for us not to be ashamed to acknowledge truth and to assimilate it from whatever source it comes to us. For him who scales the truth there is nothing of higher value than truth itself; it never cheapens nor abases him."[10]

Like the earlier civilizations of Rome and Persia the multi-faith and multi-ethnic Islamic civilization ruled by Arabs weakened eventually, and it was defeated by the Mongol invasion in the east and the Christian *reconquista* of Spain in the west. But before the lights of the Islamic civilization got snuffed out there were periods, during the half millennium between the founding of Baghdad in 762, as capital of the Abbasid Caliphate, and its pillage in 1258 by the Mongol armies, when men of learning gathered together in Baghdad's cafes and libraries rekindled the spirit of ancient Greek philosophers in their midst.

V.

At the Battle of Siffin soldiers of Mu`awiya raised on their spears sheets inscribed with passages from the Qur'an, and Ali was consequently forced to accept arbitration rather than shedding of blood. But blood was shed, and the Qur'an did not seem to offer by itself solution to problems that led to conflicts among Muslims. This was a troubling discovery for Muslims, since the Qur'an was for them the Word of God to be followed without questioning. This meant the message of the Qur'an was not transparent to everyone, and only men of greater discernment possessed the key to explain the Qur'an to the people. As a result a class of men, the *ulema* or religious scholars, emerged devoted professionally to the study and exegesis of the sacred text.

Islam does not formally require priests and monks in the ranks of believers as in Christianity, but the need to explain the Qur'an became imperative and the *ulema*, religious scholars, met this need and more. They collected the traditions of the Prophet in order to clarify the meaning of the Qur'an by reference to examples from his life, and to set the norm of proper Islamic conduct. They came to serve the Caliphs in the rapidly expanding empire as scribes, lawyers and judges, and in the role of jurists (*fuqāha*; singular *fāqih*) they constructed Shariah, or the Islamic code of laws, derived from the Qur'an and the traditions (*hadīth*) of the Prophet, by careful analogical reasoning (*qiyās*) and consensus (*ijmā`*) within their ranks.

By early second century of Islam non-Arab converts began to outnumber Arab Muslims. They brought with them their culture even as they assimilated the language and culture of Arabs. Then there were Jews and Christians or people of the Book(s) (*ahl al-Kitab*) and apart from them there were Zoroastrians, Buddhists,

Manicheans, polytheists and pagans; together they posed a different set of problem for the *ulema*, of how to explain why Muslims were so bitterly divided in sectarian conflicts when they insisted Islam was the best of religions. In this context some of the most explosive debates and disagreements relating to the Qur'an occurred.

In the aftermath of Hussein's martyrdom Arabs, who came to identify themselves as Shi'a, developed their own school of jurisprudence and theology around the notion of the rightful *Imam* and *Amir al-Mu'minīn* (leader and commander of the faithful) by descent through Ali and Fatima belonging to the House of the Prophet. Ali was the first Imam of the Shi'a, his sons Hasan and Hussein were the second and third Imams. In what became the Shi'a doctrine the Imams, as male descendants of the Prophet, were sinless and infallible (*ma`sūm*) in their religious knowledge thereby making them rightful rulers in politics and supreme guides in all spiritual affairs. Their mandate as Shi'a Imams did not depend on their actually possessing political power as a result of the martyrdom of Ali and Hussein.

The Shi'a Muslims came to believe their Imams possessed as gift from the Prophet special insight to understand and explain the inner, or hidden, meaning of the Qur'an. It meant, as this idea became doctrinal among the Shi'a, that the Qur'an carried an outward, literal, or exoteric (*zähir*) meaning for the faithful, and an inward, hidden, or esoteric (*bätin*) meaning only accessible directly to a privilege few. Among Ismaili Shi'a—a branch that split from the larger body of the Twelver Shi'a—the role of the Imam in interpreting the Qur'an for his followers was crucial in directing Ismaili Muslims adapt to changing political circumstances and this eventually resulted in the successful manner they adjusted to modernity.

Sunni Muslims, however, were the overwhelming majority brought together on the basis of maintaining religious and communal unity despite reported quarrels of the first generation of Muslims and the sectarian divisions that followed. They accepted as Caliph the man who effectively held political power, and followed the teachings of the mainstream *ulema* (religious scholars) while remaining fearful of discord and its effects on the society at large. Sunni Muslims formed the majority community, and their piety was based on the simple belief that the Qur'an was God's Word and that in reciting God's Word believed they were drawn literally nearer to God. In this sense, most Sunni Muslims are adherents of the *zähir*, or literal, meaning of the Qur'an.

In the early ninth century Baghdad a quarrel erupted among religious scholars over whether the Qur'an was the created speech of God, or the Qur'an was eternal and therefore uncreated and coeval with God. It became ultimately a theological question with philosophical implications of far reaching consequences.

The discovered works of Greek philosophers, in particular Aristotle, influenced the philosophical minded *ulema*, and among them emerged rationalist thinkers known as Mu`tazilîs. They affirmed that the truth reached through natural reasoning was not inconsistent with that of revelation and, hence, the meaning of the Qur'an could be explained rationally.

In an earlier dispute over the question of predestination and freewill, the Mu`tazilîs held the view that man had to be free to choose between what was lawful (*halal*) and forbidden (*haram*) before being judged for wrongful act. They argued since God was just, it would be unjust of Him punishing man deprived of choice or lacking in freewill. Their opponents countered God was omnipotent and omniscient, and had predetermined the course of history. For the Mu`tazilîs to state otherwise, their opponents insisted, meant limiting God's power to act as He wish.

The dispute over the Qur'an, whether it was created or uncreated, divided the *ulema*. Their quarrel became similar to the hugely divisive Christological debates in early Christianity—whether revelation (Christ) was located in the nature of Jesus's humanity or in the nature of Jesus's divinity. The Mu`tazilîs contended that in suggesting the Qur'an was uncreated, hence eternal when only God was eternal, led logically to *shîrk* or the sin of associating idolatrously something else with God. But for pious literal minded Muslims, as Marshall Hodgson explained in *The Venture of Islam*, "When His Word came to them they dare not treat it as a mere created thing to be disputed about; they must simply tremble, obey, and be grateful."[11]

The "Qur'an problem" for the Mu`tazilîs was part of a larger and more pressing challenge of defending Sunni Islam, or monotheism, by formulating a doctrine based on sound reason and defended when necessary by the authority of the Caliph. This was needed to fend off the excesses of the Shi'a claims for their Imams on the one side, the rigid literalism of the piety-minded traditionalists on the other, and the presence of trinitarian Christians and dualist Manicheans whose preaching struck at the foundation of Sunni Islam's strict monotheism.

But it was the piety-minded traditionalists who eventually prevailed over the Mu`tazilîs. The Ash`arîs, after the religious scholar Abul Hasan al-Ash`arî (d. 935), countered the rationalist Mu`tazilîs on behalf of the piety-minded traditionalists with an anti-rationalist theology that eventually ended any form of speculative philosophy within mainstream Sunni Islam.

The Ash`arîs declared God's power was unlimited and His will was inscrutable. God could neither be defined nor explained by human reason, and any such attempt was tantamount to insulting God. Moreover, any effort to bind God with the notion of justice, or any other attribute was, in itself, contrary to the Mu`tazilî view, a sinful act. The Ash`arî theology buttressed the literalism of the piety-minded traditionalists that tended towards anthropomorphism, and which greatly offended the rational-minded Mu`tazilîs.

The Sunni Caliphs in Baghdad eventually adopted the Ash`arî theology (*kalām*) as the orthodox doctrine of the mainstream Sunni Islam. But the debate between the two schools, the traditionalists and the rationalists, continued until it was exhausted toward the end of the twelfth century and finally ended with the Mongol invasion that left Baghdad in ruins. The list of men involved in the debates—al-Kindi, al-Farabi, Ibn Sina (Avicenna), Ghazali (Algazel), Ibn Rushd (Averroës)—were among the most illustrious in the Islamic civilization before Europe's rebirth. In this honor list of names that of Ghazali, bestowed by his peers with the title of *Hujjat al-Islam* (the "Proof of Islam"), was greatly revered by Sunni Muslims.

vi.

Abu Hamid Muhammad Ghazali (1058-1111) was of Persian origin, as was Abu Ali al-Husain Ibn Sina, or Avicenna (980-1037) in Latin. Ghazali was a Sunni Muslim before Persians under the Safavid rulers after 1500 were converted to Shi'a Islam. About Ibn Sina there persists some controversy as to the sect of Islam he belonged. In an autobiography Ibn Sina dictated to one of his pupils, he indicated his father had been won over to the Ismaili sect and, more than likely, he followed his father secretly while serving the Sunni authorities of his time.

Ibn Sina's philosophical speculations marked the apogee of rationalism in all of Islam spurred by the works of Greek philosophers, most notably Aristotle. He ridiculed the literalism of piety-minded traditionalists, and wrote the true happiness of philosophers resided in the quest for spiritual perfection. This recalled Aristotle's view in *The Nicomachean Ethics* (Book Ten) that "the activity of God, which is supremely happy, must be a form of contemplation; and therefore among human activities that which is most akin to God's will be the happiest."[12]

Whatever the merits of Ibn Sina's speculations, among common people philosophy (*falsafāh*) raised doubts in matters of belief; similarly theology (*kalām*), as the Qur'an problem illustrated, fueled quarrels over God's nature when for the piety-minded traditionalists there was no room in Islam for any doubt on God's unity and majesty. The only subject worthy of study while avoiding controversy was *fiqh* (jurisprudence), and among learned Muslims serious individuals were taken to be the *fuqāha* or jurists responsible for the development of the Islamic law or Shariah. Instead of sowing doubts the jurists, unlike the philosophers in the opinion of common Muslims, contributed to happiness by guiding people on the right path and assuring them paradise in the afterlife.

Ghazali studied jurisprudence and his merits earned him appointment as director of the prestigious Nizamiyyah *madrasāh* (school) in Baghdad by Nizam ul-Mulk, vizir or chief minister of the ruling Seljuq Sultan. Seljuq warriors of Turkish origin had reduced the Abbasid Caliphs by the eleventh century to nominal authority, and decline of the Abbasid Caliphate hastened the fragmentation of central power. It fell to men like Ghazali to defend the mainstream orthodox Sunni Islam in troubled times, and keep firm the faith of the common piety-minded traditionalist Muslims.

Ghazali was celebrated for turning the tools of philosophers—reason and logic—against them. In his well-known response to Ibn Sina, *Tahâfut al-falâsifah* ("The Incoherence of the Philosophers"), Ghazali argued that though logic worked for mathematics and in solving theorems, when applied to metaphysics it led to incoherence. He insisted revelation was not bound, nor explicable, by reason, and that belief in religion required unquestioning faith.

With Ghazali came the triumph of Ash`arî theology. The rearguard effort of Ibn Rushd (1126-1198), the most eminent commentator of Aristotle's work among Muslims, in *Tahâfut al-Tahâfut* ("The Incoherence of the Incoherence") written in response to Ghazali, came late and had no lasting effect in dislodging literalism in mainstream Sunni thinking. After Ghazali was done with his attack on philosophy, the philosophers within majority Sunni Islam went silent. Ibn Rushd's effort, instead, found enthusiasts among Christian scholars—Thomas Aquinas (1225-1274) was one among them—and their Scholasticism eventually succeeded with support of the Church in reconciling revelation and reason within Christianity.

Ash`arî theology was a precursor of nominalism that surfaced in the theology of churchmen Duns Scotus (d. 1308) and William of Ockham (1285-1347). Aristotle had taught that God as the Unmoved Mover arranged the universe according to natural law, which meant there were "universals" as "genera" and "species", and "particulars" were instances of the "universals". It was the task of philosophers to discover the working of natural law through cause and effect of things and events, and God therefore could be explained by the study of His creation. But Ghazali rejected Aristotelian rationalism in matters of faith, as did the nominalists. According to Michael Gillespie in *The Theological Origins of Modernity*, "If there are no universals, every being must be radically individual, a unique creation of God himself, called forth out of nothing by his infinite power and sustained by that power alone."[13]

For Christian nominalists and for Ghazali before them, the defense of God's omnipotence as unlimited power led them to conceive God as pure will. God acts as He pleases, William of Ockham argued in similar manner as Ghazali had done, since man's reasoning or wishes do not bind Him. William pushed the nominalist argument against the Scholastics beyond absurdity to make his point of God as pure will by declaring, as Gillespie noted, God "did not even have to send his son in the form of a man; the savior might have been a donkey or a rock."[14]

In medieval Christianity nominalism generated a passing crisis, which the Scholastics met armed with Aristotelian rationalism and the Church suppressed it. In Sunni Islam the work of Ghazali, as a precursor of nominalism, instead armed the orthodoxy to punish philosophers as heretics. In the realm of politics, the unchallenged supremacy of Ash`arî theology—God as pure will—readily provided tyrants in the world of Islam with a patina of religious legitimacy.

The jurists of Sunni Islam reached a consensus after Ghazali and declared the doors of independent reasoning or inquiry (*ijtihād*) closed. In their view Shariah was complete leaving room only for imitation (*taqlīd*) by the *ulema* of rulings already established. This meant the overwhelming majority of mainstream Muslims was locked within the religious framework of Sunni orthodoxy as devised by religious scholars of late antiquity and early medieval era, and since then confined to live in denial or ignorance of new sciences and their effects on the sum total of human knowledge.

vii.

In a lecture given at the Sorbonne, Paris, on "Islam and Science" in March 1883, Ernest Renan, a French expert on Semitic languages and civilizations, observed,

> Shortly after the year 1200 or thereabouts, there is no longer a single renowned Arab philosopher. Philosophy had always been persecuted within Islam, but in a way that hadn't been successful in suppressing it. From 1200, the theological reaction prevails completely. Philosophy is abolished in Muslim countries... From that period onward, with few exceptions such as Ibn Khaldun, Islam will no longer be broadminded; it has killed science and philosophy in its midst.[15]

Ghazali's role in this reaction was significant.

But there was another dimension in Ghazali's life that was also significant. He had an acute mid-life crisis with personal doubts relating to his work as teacher and jurist. Following the assassination of his mentor Nizam ul-Mulk in 1092, Ghazali left his post in Baghdad and found for himself secret refuge in Damascus and later Jerusalem. When Ghazali returned from his retirement after overcoming his inner doubts, he devoted his remaining years in teaching what he had learned by immersing himself in the Sufi path of the "other Islam" in contrast to the legalistic, or political, Islam of the orthodoxy.

Ghazali's reputation brought attention among Sunni Muslims to his effort in harmonizing orthodox Islam based on Shariah, and Sufism based on the path (*tariqāh*) of seeking inner illumination in the quest of God. Until Ghazali Sunni *ulema* in general were suspicious of Sufis, and considered them at best deviant. Sufism was officially discouraged despite its popularity, and the example made of the Sufi devotee Mansur al-Hallaj publicly executed in 922 on order of the authorities in Baghdad stood as a warning.

During the post-crisis phase of his life, Ghazali composed two books that just about repudiated his earlier writings. In *Mishkat al-Anwar* ("The Niche for Lights") and *Jawahir al-Quran* ("The Jewels of the Quran") Ghazali expressed his revised understanding of the Qur'an on learning of its hidden meaning based on his mystical experiences. He conceded that the literal reading of the Qur'an was insufficient, even mistaken, for God's Word was largely allegorical. The Qur'an in its self-description, according to Ghazali, was like an ocean vast and deep, and jewels hidden therein were not readily accessible without earnest search and investment of great effort in seeking the eternal truth.

In *Mishkat* Ghazali expounded on the celebrated "Light-Verse" (24:35) of the Qur'an by adopting the "Veils Tradition" of Sufis. The verse, a favourite of the mystics in Islam, reads:

> God is the Light of the heavens and the earth;
> the likeness of His Light is as a niche
>   wherein is a lamp
> (the lamp is a glass,
> the glass as it were a glittering star)
> kindled from a Blessed Tree,
> an olive that is neither of the East nor of the West
> whose oil wellnigh would shine, even if no fire touched it;
>   Light upon Light;

(God guides to His Light whom He will.)

Ghazali meditated on "light" as a heavenly metaphor illuminating the material world. Then inspired by Sufi mystics, he dwelled upon the meaning of "light" by reference to human intelligence or "reason", followed by the hidden knowledge of saints, prophets, and celestial entities made manifest by "light" emanating from God and, finally, on God alone—for God being the only source of "light" and the only real "light", or "light" in itself, exists everlastingly.

Sufi influence on Ghazali was made evident in the *Mishkat*. He was also greatly influenced by Neoplatonism of al-Farabi (c. 872-950)—revered as the "Second Master", Aristotle being the first, by philosophers who came after him, including Moses Maimonides (1135-1204)—and Ibn Sina, even though Ghazali did not mention their names in the *Mishkat*. Indeed, without formal acknowledgement Ghazali was walking in the shadow of Mansur al-Hallaj. As A.J. Wensinck, Ghazali's modern interpreter, has written, "The doctrine of Ghazali is Semitic monotheism seen through the prism of Neo-Platonism."[16] But Ghazali, aware of the hazard into which Mansur al-Hallaj fell, prudently stopped short of openly denouncing Ash`ari theology that he had once so zealously embraced.

In *Jawahir* Ghazali assembled some fifteen hundred verses, nearly a quarter of the Qur'an, as jewels and discussed their hidden meaning. It is noteworthy that Ghazali excluded from his collection those verses most readily cited by Islamists, especially verses from Chapter 9 titled *al-Tawbah* or "Repentance", and known as the "sword verses". In *Milestones* Qutb gave priority to these verses in his scheme for the revival of Islam, and these verses are cited by jihadists of al-Qaeda, Hamas, Hezbollah, Taliban, Isis, Boko Haram *et al* as the source for justifying their indiscriminate criminal violence and terrorism. For Ghazali, however, the Sufi notion of inner illumination in the quest for God and truth was the defining criterion in selecting the "jewel" verses. He wrote,

> The truth is that the seeker and the Sought are comparable to a picture present in a mirror: The picture is not revealed in it because of rust on its surface; when, however, you polish the mirror the picture is revealed in it, neither by the movement of the picture towards it nor by its movement towards the picture, but by the removal of the veil. God (may He be exalted) is revealed by His essence and is not concealed, for concealment of light is impossible, and by light everything which is concealed becomes obvious, and God is the light of the heavens and the earth.[17]

The legacy of Ghazali, according to Robert Reilly in *The Closing of the Muslim Mind,* was that he left Muslims as intellectual orphans by depriving them of the learning Aristotle had bequeathed to the world. On the contrary, Ghazali's legacy has remained paradoxical. In his late embrace of Sufism, Ghazali offered a tantalizing glimpse of the promise he saw in the "other Islam" to exit out of the box, or coffin, into which at first he had placed himself and his people as the most celebrated exponent of Ash`ari theology.

viii.

Toward the end of the eleventh century the Middle East began to slide into upheaval of the sort that has come to characterize the region beginning in the second half of the twentieth century. Christendom launched Crusades to recover lost holy lands, which brought increasing pressures on both Sunni Caliphs of the Abbasid dynasty in Baghdad and Ismaili Shi'a Caliphs of the Fatimid dynasty in Cairo.

Within a few decades after Ghazali's death in 1111 disorder in the Middle East began to take its toll. The Fatimid Empire in North Africa, ruled by Ismaili Shi'a Imams claiming descent from the Prophet through his daughter Fatima (hence, Fatimid), disintegrated and its last ruler was replaced by Salah-al-Din (Saladin), a Sunni warlord of Kurdish origin in 1171. Salah-al-Din reorganized the Arab armies of Egypt and led them to "liberate" Jerusalem from the Crusaders.

Ismaili Shi'a Muslims were dispersed across the Middle East and beyond. The Mongols eventually destroyed their military strongholds in the mountains around the Caspian Sea. It was ironical that defeats suffered by the Ismaili Imams emancipated them from the burden of political rule, and when forced into hiding and exile they were limited to minister only to the spiritual needs of their followers. Somewhat similar to Jews defeated and dispersed to live as a minority among Christians and later Muslims, Ismaili Shi'a Muslims acquired the knowledge and talents to become adept in accommodating change while remaining faithful to their esoteric belief. Ismaili Muslims led by their Imams—the Aga Khans claiming direct descent from the Prophet—eventually adapted to the setting of the modern secular world, and their example is indicative there is no dogma within Islam that forbids Muslims in embracing modernity.

The Crusaders were defeated by Muslims and expelled from the holy lands, but the Mongol invasion destroyed the Abbasid rule. In 1258 Hulagu, a grandson of Genghis Khan, surrounded Baghdad at the head of his Mongol armies. The Abbasid Caliph al-Musta`sim had refused an earlier invitation by Hulagu to join forces with the Mongols against the remnants of the Ismaili warlords and their dreaded ranks of *assassins*—forerunners of the *jihādi* "suicide bombers" that plague contemporary Islam—in their Caspian strongholds.

As Hulagu and his Mongol warriors prepared to storm Baghdad, the inhabitants of the Abbasid capital feared the end of time had arrived for them. Al-Musta`sim surrendered unconditionally when Hulagu entered Baghdad, and pleaded for his life. The Caliph of Islam, instead, was bundled in a carpet on the orders of Hulagu and trampled to death. Baghdad was torched, its famed libraries desecrated, its learned men put to death or forced to flee, and Arab rule over Muslims ceased for nearly seven centuries until in the aftermath of World War I the victorious powers over the Ottoman Turks—Britain and France—in mapping the modern boundaries of the Middle East created Arab states of Lebanon, Syria, Jordan, Iraq, Kuwait, Saudi Arabia, and the Gulf Emirates.

ix.

The intellectual orphans of Ghazali in Sunni Islam were left in despair to make sense of their world after the Mongol destruction of Baghdad. Hulagu embraced Islam and his Mongol warriors joined the ranks of Muslims, but the Turks eventually prevailed over the Mongols and ended their rule over the Middle East. Between the Mongols and the Turks the Caliphs of Islam were reduced to mere nominal figureheads controlled by the armies of contending warlords in the region. In such circumstances the question that agitated the *ulema* was to whom belonged the loyalty of Muslims as representative and successor of the Prophet.

One among the intellectual orphans of Ghazali beginning to populate Sunni Islam ever since was Taqi al-Din Ibn Taymiyya (1263-1328). He was born to a Damascene family of Hanbali scholars devoted to the school of Ahmad ibn Hanbal (780-855), a noted reporter-compiler of *hadīth* (the Prophetic traditions) and a legist of deeply conservative bent of mind. Ibn Hanbal had a devoted following among piety-minded Sunni Muslims, and he was revered for his defiance, despite imprisonment and reports of maltreatment by the orders of the Abbasid Caliph Al-Mamun (ruled 813-833), in rejecting the Mu`tazilî view of the Qur'an as God's created speech, which was at the time official doctrine.

Ibn Taymiyya's outlook as a rigid dogmatist was shaped in the aftermath of the Mongol sack of Baghdad. He found himself, as a Hanbali legist, immersed in the debate on how to settle upon the right definition of a Muslim, since the Mongols professed Islam yet preferred to rule by their own inherited law code instead of Shariah. The Mongols also ranked loyalty to their Khanate above loyalty to Islam.

Ibn Taymiyya preached *jihād* against the Mongol authorities, and defended the doctrine of *takfīr*, or passing judgment on Muslims as heretics or apostates over differences on religious issues. His insistence on pronouncing *takfīr* on other Muslims (Shi'a, Ismaili, Sufi, including Sunni traditionalists tolerant of others) irritated the authorities. He was imprisoned on several occasions and at the end died in prison.

Ibn Taymiyya became known for the innovative use of referring to the *salāf* (those so-called "righteous" ancestors belonging to the first three generations after the Prophet) in theological disputes over how to interpret the verses of the Qur'an. He reasoned the *salāfi* understanding and practice of Islam by necessity was superior to that of later generations of Muslims, and in pushing the idea of "salafism" (revival of the "imaginary" pristine Islam) he also devised another weapon against philosophy and philosophers within Sunni Islam.

Ibn Taymiyya's *salāf*-based legalism repudiated as heresy any independent intellectual effort (*ijtihād*) in the exegesis of the Qur'an. The doctrine of "salafism" implied Muslims defiled God's Word when they allowed alien ideas—for example, pagan-Greek philosophy—to seduce them. *Salāfism* became a rebuke of Muslims failing to practice "authentic" Islam defined by the conduct of the *salāf* and which, consequently, invited God's wrath as punishment signified by the ruinous Mongol invasion of the House of Islam. A return to "salafism" meant repentance (*taw'ba*) for deviating from "authentic Islam" as practiced by the *salāf* and strict compliance with Shariah, particularly those rulings compiled by Ibn Hanbal and his associates.

In the decades after Ibn Taymiyya's death Turkish tribes in the Middle East consolidated their power, captured Constantinople in

1453, and brought the seat of the Caliphate to the Byzantine capital renamed Istanbul. The Ottoman Turks, as Caliphs of Sunni Islam and Sultans of the Ottoman Empire, ruled through the age of gunpowder empires into the modern era when Britain and France defeated them during World War I of 1914-18.

But in the arid and primitive interior of Arabia and out of reach of the rulers in Istanbul, Muhammad ibn Abd al-Wahhab (1703-1792) took Ibn Taymiyya as a forerunner in launching his own version of nominalist theology based on God as pure will. He pronounced *takfīr* on Muslims he found disagreeable, and readily declared *jihād* against them. He cursed Shi'a Muslims as unbelievers, instructed his followers to demolish shrines of saintly Sufi teachers where common folks gathered to honor their memory, and preached a return to the "imagined" pristine Islam of the *salāf*. After him Wahhabism mutated into an ideology in search of political power, and eventually the Wahhabi *ulema* in partnership with Abdulaziz ibn Saud (1875-1953) and his tribe established the Kingdom of Saudi Arabia following World War I.

X.

The "other Islam" right from the outset of Muslim history stood at the opposite end of political Islam, or Islamism. Those among the Prophet's companions who were distressed by the persistence of tribalism, even while Muhammad preached unity of the faithful as the ideal for the new community under his leadership, drifted away into anonymity after his death. Some were early converts, others acquired notice as the Prophet's close associates, but apart from very few of those companions most disappeared without any mention of their names from that early decades of Islamic history.

Among few names that later generations remembered for their piety were those of Bilal, Abu Dharr, and Salman al-Farsi. They shared in common their outsider status for not belonging to any of the principal tribes in Mecca or Medina, or to any subsidiary clans of those tribes. In the intra-tribal conflicts that broke out after Muhammad's death they remained neutral, if not distant. But it was unlikely they were alone in their distress with the political violence that erupted even as the Prophet lay ill and dying in Medina.

It was with these early companions of the Prophet, who walked away from any prominent role in the public life of the first Muslim community in Islamic history, that we might trace the beginnings of the "other Islam" as distinct from political Islam. They eschewed politics, or the pursuit of power in the name of Islam, for a quiet life of contemplation, prayers, and simple living. They beheld in the Prophet the perfect embodiment of a man devoted to God and who was described in the Qur'an as a contemplative soul. The word "Sufi", according to many who have written about Sufism, was derived from the word "suf" meaning "wool", and as "Sufis" these followers of Muhammad and devotees of God wore coarse woollen clothes indicative of their simple and unostentatious living.

The "other Islam" was infused by the mystical quest of the believers seeking union with the One addressed as the Ever Compassionate. The name Hasan of Basra stands at the head of the earliest Sufis, or the mystics in Islam. From the biographical notes on Sufis (known as "Memorial of the Saints") compiled by Farid al-Din Attar, a beloved Persian poet of the thirteenth century, we learn Hasan was born in 642 in Medina, some ten years after Muhammad's death, and died in Basra, Iraq, in 728. He grew up among the earliest companions of the Prophet, witnessed the fratricidal wars that ended with the making of the Umayyad Caliphate in Damascus, withdrew from any involvement in politics, and was widely respected for his piety and wisdom.

The Sufis became in time the visible counterpoint to political Islam, and as their reputation spread they also became the standard bearers of Islam as the "religion of peace" in a world filled with conflicts. What set the Sufis apart from the *ulema*, who formed the bulwark of the political order of the Caliphate, was their reading of the Qur'an and, accordingly, the life to be lived inspired by such reading that was remarkably different from the exegesis of the Qur'an by Islamists of the past and present.

The Islam of the Sufis has remained inspirational to a vast majority of Muslims providing them with an ethically compelling example of quiet devotion and spiritually meaningful living in a world beset with troubles. It might be said that the Sufi version of Islam thrives despite the ruins spread by political Islam. The Sufis understand that the meaning of the Qur'an is as intricate and layered as the woven threads of a Persian carpet, and that the Qur'an's hidden meaning is infinite yet eternally fresh for the unborn generations. Here are a few verses, as examples, from the Qur'an cherished in Sufi circles.

> Though all the trees in the earth were
> pens, and the sea – seven seas after it
> to replenish it,
> yet would the Words of God not be spent.
> God is All-mighty, All-wise (31:27).
>
> We indeed created man; and We know
> what his soul whispers within him,
> and We are nearer to him than the
> jugular vein (50:15).
>
> And when My servants question thee
> concerning Me – I am near to answer
> the calls of the caller, when he calls
> to Me; so let them respond to me,
> and let them believe in Me; haply so
> they will go aright (2:182).

Two of the most revered mystics of Islam were Muhyi-uddin Ibn `Arabi (1165-1240) and Jalaluddin Rumi (1207-1273). Ibn `Arabi was from the *maghreb* (the west) born in Murcia, Spain, and Rumi was from the *mashreq* (the east) born in Balkh,

Afghanistan. They were contemporaries during the time of the Mongol invasion of the Middle East, and in the midst of the great upheaval their writings illuminated a path for believers seeking inner tranquility in a conflict-ridden world. There is a vast amount of their writings available in translation, and much has been written about both as mystics, poets, theosophists, scholars, and sages. What is of interest here is their role as teachers of what the "other Islam" means, and how it is distinctly different from political Islam, or Islamism.

The foundational principle in Ibn `Arabi's teaching was the notion of oneness, implying inclusiveness, based on his main theme of the "Unity" or the "Oneness of Being" expressed as *wahdat al-wūjud.* According to Ralph Austin in his introduction to Ibn `Arabi's *The Bezels of Wisdom*, this "Oneness of Being" suggests "all distinction, difference, and conflict are but apparent facets of a single and unique reality."[18] In the mystic's view there was only the One Reality, God, and all else was His manifestation, as in the widely quoted saying of the Sufis about God, "I was a hidden treasure who longed to be known; therefore I created the world." In the mysticism of Ibn `Arabi the "other" was inseparable from the One, as all separateness dissolved in the eternal reality of God. The subject-object duality, in Ibn `Arabi's teaching, was merely apparent, or deceptive, since both were intimately bound and together reflected the infinitude of expressions or manifestations of the One; it therefore meant that the many religions, despite their different history and the varying experiences of each religion's founder or prophet as exemplar of virtue, wisdom and excellence in conduct, were so many pathways leading ultimately to the One.

Ibn `Arabi left his native city for travelling to the east and eventually settled in Damascus, Syria. He found himself surrounded by Ghazali's intellectual orphans hurling anathemas on people of different faiths or sects, since the "other" to them was real or potential enemy. But denial of the "other" as non-believer, or infidel, which has been the hallmark of Islamism was inconceivable in the esotericism of Ibn `Arabi. For Ibn `Arabi the "other", just as oneself, represented an image or form of the One to love and revere. He wrote:

> O Marvel! A garden amidst the flames.
> My heart has become capable of every form:
> It is a pasture for gazelles and a convent for Christian monks,
> and a temple for idols and the pilgrim's Kaa'ba,
> and the tables of the Torah and the book of the Koran.
> I follow the religion of Love: whatever way Love's camels take,
> that is my religion and my faith.

Ibn `Arabi was fondly addressed as Shayk al-Akbar, or the "Greatest Master."[19] Similarly, Jalaluddin Rumi's followers named him "Maulana", meaning "our Master," and his didactic poems in the collection called *Mathnawï* has been cherished and memorized ever since by Persian (Farsi) speaking people, as spiritual expressions of the highest order. Jami, a poet in fifteenth century Herat, the Timurid capital located in present day Afghanistan, expressed the widely held view about Rumi's writings in a couplet of his own:

> *Mathnawï-yi maulawï ma`nawï*
> *hast Qur'an dar zabän-i-pahlawï*
>
> (The spiritual couplets of Maulana
> are the Qur'an in the Persian tongue.)

Jalaluddin's parents had migrated from Balkh to Konya in Anatolia (modern Turkey), known at the time as *Rüm*, or Roman, and which he adopted as his pen name. For Rumi, like Ibn Arabi, the eternal truth was contained in the verse of the Qur'an: "All that dwells upon the earth is perishing, yet still abides the Face of thy Lord, majestic, splendid" (55:26). The mystic current, which illuminated the lives of Ibn Arabi and Rumi, runs as a thread through all religions and holds them together like a necklace.

Islam was, for Ibn Arabi and Rumi, one among many pathways for a seeker of God through prayers and remembrance (*dhikr*) finding Him present within oneself, for as the Qur'an promises "We are nearer to him than the jugular vein."

In *Fïhi mä fïhi* Rumi expressed in his inimitable style, which might be likened to a Zen-like slap, on how to read and comprehend a sacred text, in this case the Qur'an:

> The Koran is a two-sided brocade. Some enjoy the one side, some the other. Both are true and correct, as God Most High wishes that both groups might have use from it. In the same way, a woman has a husband and a baby; each of them enjoys her in a different way. The child's pleasure comes from her bosom and her milk, that of the husband from kisses and sleeping and embrace. Some people are children on the path and drink milk—these enjoy the external meaning of the Koran. But those who are true men know of another enjoyment and have a different understanding of the inner meanings of the Koran.[20]

In describing the Qur'an as a woman who provides care differently for her child and her husband, Rumi offered a radical view of the Qur'an, or of its Author, as being feminine in nature, while indicating that the reading of a sacred text is inseparable from the psychology of the reader and what the reader brings to the text. Rumi taught the Qur'an could not be turned into a closed book, or the meaning of the Qur'an fixed by the dictate of any one authority and imposed on everyone else. It was a lesson the Qur'an itself indicated, as in the verse referring to "trees as pens" and "seven seas" as ink and yet God's Word as colloquy is limitless; or, as in the verse in which the Prophet remarks, "O my Lord, behold, my people have taken this Koran as a thing to be shunned" (25:30), meaning they fettered it without understanding its message.

For both Ibn Arabi and Rumi what was true in Islam was also true in other faith traditions, and the learning they imparted to Muslims was to draw equally upon the wisdom of other traditions, while dissolving the walls of separateness between oneself and the other. According to Annemarie Schimmel in *Mystical Dimensions of Islam,*

> Greek and Christian traditions were very much alive in Konya in the thirteenth century. The old centers of Cappadocian Christianity and the large monastic settlement in the caves near Göreme were only a few days' journey from the capital. Thus images alluding to Jesus and Mary occur more frequently in Jalaluddin's poetry than in any other comparable poetical work, though such allusions are common in Muslim poetry.[21]

The orthodox Sunni Muslims remained suspicious of Ibn `Arabi and Rumi, since they viewed their widespread influence as harmful in weakening the common Muslim's strict adherence to Shariah. But the tender appeal of Sufis to follow the longings of the heart and seek God within could not be denied, and the Sufi version of Islam spread into regions remote from the Middle East. Once political Islam started crumbling before the weight of the European powers in the latter half of the eighteenth century, the Sufi tradition became largely responsible in maintaining Islam as a culture beyond the shrinking frontiers of the Ottoman Empire.

But the immense attraction of Sufism meant, as in all things human, charlatans and poseurs as holy men exploiting the weak, the gullible, and the vulnerable among Muslims and non-Muslims alike. The Sunni orthodoxy in frequently denouncing such corruption generated counter-Sufi movements heralding conservative reform. The anti-Sufi argument of the orthodoxy was Sufism weakened Muslims from within to resist and defeat enemies of Islam. Yet the influence of Sufism over time was so widespread that conservative reformers ironically had to adopt Sufi norms to convince common Muslims their effort was directed only against corruption and abuse that had seeped into Islam masquerading as Sufism.

xi.

Civilizations are not insular; they are, instead, result of the mixing of cultures. The Islamic civilization was a result of this mixing right from the outset when Arabs of the desert burst into history in the seventh century. Within a few decades of the Prophet's death in 632 the political capital of Muslims was moved from Medina in Arabia to Damascus, a Byzantine city in Syria, by Mu`awiya of the Umayyad clan in Mecca. The Abbasid revolution moved the political capital from Damascus to Baghdad less than a century later where the Persian influence was most felt. The Ottoman Turks moved the political capital some seven centuries later to Istanbul (formerly Constantinople), which was built by the Emperor Constantine as the seat of the Eastern Roman Empire or Byzantine.

The Islamic civilization at its high noon—between the eighth century and the thirteenth century—and before the Mongol invasion was a "melting pot" of Byzantine and Persian cultures around the Mediterranean. From this perspective, it might be said, the Mediterranean was the "Sea of Abraham"—the only body of water surrounded by cultures whose people despite differences in ethnicity and their quarrels turned to the same God of Abraham in prayer.

Islam as a civilization absorbed those that preceded it. Fernand Braudel in *A History of Civilizations* observed, "As Christianity inherited from the Roman Empire of which it was a prolongation, so Islam instantly took hold of the Near East, perhaps the oldest crossroads of civilized humanity." And in terms of faith, Braudel observed, "even in its religion Islam is linked with Judaism and Christianity, with the family of Abraham, and with the Old Testament and its rigorous monotheism."[22]

The mixing in the Indian subcontinent was between Islam of the Near East with its center in Baghdad and the Hindu-Buddhist civilization, which had emerged more than a millennium before the Common Era in the lands between the Indus and the Ganges. In the distant islands of Southeast Asia (modern Indonesia) Islam came into contact with the Javanese culture, and there evolved as a result a hybrid Indonesian culture of Islam through mixing with the local traditions.

But civilizations also wither, crack, and disintegrate. History is filled with records of civilizations that once thrived and then eventually perished. A partial explanation for a civilization disintegrating is the loss of its capacity to respond effectively in adapting over time to the challenges it faces from within and from the outside.

From about early thirteenth century the Islamic civilization began losing its inner plasticity to accommodate ideas, especially in the realm of philosophy, with implications for the ruling political culture within the House of Islam. Once the intellectual orphans of Ghazali dogmatically declared speculative philosophy forbidden (*haram*), they pulled the curtains on the Islamic civilization and denounced any openness on the part of Muslims to new ideas or innovations as heresy (*bid'āh*). The rigid conservatism of the *ulema* became the death rattle of the Islamic civilization.

As Europe's Renaissance zigzagged through the wars of the Reformation and Counter-Reformation into the Age of Enlightenment and the making of the modern age of scientific revolution with accompanying political reforms, the House of Islam faded into intellectual obscurity and cultural poverty. All that was left among Muslims was periodic futile rebellions, as evidence of the *rigor mortis* of a dying civilization, against European powers acquiring political control over lands of the House of Islam.

But Europeans, despite their amazing advances, proved that Europe was not immune from the malady of civilizations self-destructing. The two world wars, the Holocaust and mass murders, in the first half of the twentieth century were massively self-destructive for Europe as the cradle of modernity. One of the unintended consequences of Europe's malady of self-destruction in the twentieth century was bringing down the curtains on its overseas empires, and with it came the re-emergence of the House of Islam as independent states in North Africa, the Middle East, and South and Southeast Asia. Muslims however were unprepared politically to assume responsibilities as citizens of independent states, and culturally to assimilate the new realities of the modern world. For nearly five hundred years their somnambulance through history had left them incapable to accommodate modernity and adapt to its demands.

Muslims, however, cannot opt out of the modern world and history. Their reactionary resistance, as exemplified by Khomeini and the 1979 revolution in Iran, might have temporarily succeeded in holding back modernity. In the longer term such resistance is retrograde, and Muslim societies consequently appear to the rest of the world as bizarre outposts of medievalism.

xii.

The intellectual orphans of Ghazali were bound to mount a fierce resistance to modernity and derail the efforts of Muslim modernizers. The "clash of interpretations"—in the apt description of the Franco-Tunisian scholar Abdelwahab Meddeb (1946-2014)—within Islam turning violent between advocates of political Islam and Muslim modernizers was predictable.

In *The Malady of Islam* (originally published as *La Maladie de l'Islam* in 2002), Meddeb analyzed the "crisis of Islam" spilling over into the twenty-first century as pathology not uncommon in history. He wrote, "If fanaticism was the sickness in Catholicism, if Nazism was the sickness in Germany, then surely fundamentalism is the sickness in Islam."[23] By "fundamentalism" Meddeb meant the dogmatism that leads to splitting the world into "pure" and "impure", and that the "impure" needs to be expunged to protect the "pure." In *Islam and the Challenge of Civilization*, Meddeb discussed the lethal consequences of this urge among fundamentalist Muslims to purge the "impure" that turned into violent inquisitions within the Muslim world against those who fail or refuse to abide by their narrow and inflexible dogma of Islam.

"In his zeal to purify Islam," Meddeb wrote about Ibn Taymiyya, "he turned nihilist, negating civilizing elements for the sake of religious rules, thereby ridding the religion of all those elements that had acclimatized Islam to so many cultures that it shared, and that had kept at bay the temptation to turn inward on itself."[24] Ibn Taymiyya's *salāfism* in effect became the fundamentalist creed of Ghazali's intellectual orphans—an empty shell of rituals and legalism that exercised their fanaticism even as they turned inward against the world they barely comprehended.

Some six centuries after Ibn Taymiyya came Sayyid Qutb. In *Milestones*, the most widely read textbook on political Islam, Qutb declared "every aspect of life should be under the sovereignty of God, and those who rebel against God's sovereignty and usurp it for themselves should be opposed."[25] The *salāfism* of Ibn Taymiyya had logically morphed into *jihādism* of Sayyid Qutb, and with it political Islam reached its doctrinal *cul-de-sac* in the middle years of the twentieth century.

But Muslim modernizers proved unprepared both in understanding the complex challenges ahead of them in modernizing their societies and in responding credibly to those who turned Islam into a totalitarian ideology. They were handicapped by their nationalist ideology learned from European politics without figuring out how to reconcile traditional Islam with modern secular nationalism. And when confronted with Zionism as a successful Jewish nationalist movement, the Arab modernizers failed to oppose the vitriolic anti-Jew bigotry of the Mufti of Jerusalem, Haj Amin al-Husseini (1895-1974), and the movement he launched as *jihād* against Jews in Palestine at the end of World War I.

The period following the defeat of the Ottoman Empire in 1918 offered an historic opportunity to modernizers for pushing the reform of Islam. It was for them to explain to Muslims how they would be judged in history for failing culturally in responding creatively relative to others, how they could not opt out of the modern world, and how the *salāfi* juxtaposition of an idealized early Islam with the modern world and their wish to return to it led to a dead end. For Muslim modernizers the task of reconciling Islam with the modern world required re-discovering the Mu`tazilî rationalism and reading the Qur'an in the light of the "other Islam." This was not an impossible task. The wind of history was on their back. As nationalists they embraced the idea of the modern nation-state and found in the Qur'an support in the verse, "O mankind, We have created you male and female, and appointed you races and tribes, that you may know one another" (49:13).

The path of "other Islam" is inclusive of others, of seeing in others reflection of oneself and one's own needs and aspirations. There can be no righteousness among Muslims by denying the rights of others.

In embracing nationalism as the basis of gaining independence from European colonial rule, it was incumbent on Muslim modernizers to recognize national rights of others among them, especially people of minority faith—for instance, of Jews in the case of their historic rights in Palestine—and through mutual recognition work together for just settlement where contending nationalisms collided.

The pitfall the Mufti of Jerusalem and his people dug for Arabs, and Muslims in general, in denying the historic rights of Jews in Palestine was in perverting Islam and violating the Qur'an that bears witness to those rights. The Qur'an might rightly be described as the scripture revealed to Muhammad, which narrates the history of Jews to pagan Arabs for their edification. And there are several references in the Qur'an that speaks of Jews as guided, or directed, to reside in land described as holy, as in the following verse:

> And when Moses said to his people,
> 'O my people, remember God's blessing
> upon you, when He appointed among you
> Prophets, and appointed you kings, and gave you
> Such as He had not given to any being.
> O my people, enter the Holy Land
> which God has prescribed for you, and turn not
> back in your traces, to turn about losers' (v. 5:20).

The surrender of modernizers among Arabs to the virulent anti-Jew bigotry of the Mufti was the slippery slope for Muslims that took them down into the dead end of political Islam. Similarly, in undivided India of the British Raj the push by Muslim nationalists for a separate state of Pakistan was the beginning of the end of the modernizing reformist movement among that segment of India's Muslim population who sought a synthesis between traditional Islam and modern philosophy, as in the works of Sir Sayyid Ahmad Khan (1817-1898), Sir Muhammad Iqbal (1877-1938), and Maulana Abul Kalam Azad (1888-1958).[26]

The inability of modernizers to push back Ghazali's intellectual orphans in the ranks of the *ulema* and among political activists mobilized by the example of the Mufti of Jerusalem, reflected their unpreparedness in the realm of ideas and religion to counter the bigotry of political Islam on the basis of the "other Islam." They failed to educate Muslims how, for instance, Sayyid Qutb and other advocates of political Islam, twisted the Qur'an into a neo-pagan text of bloodlust and indiscriminate warfare against everyone who rejected their *jihādi* reading of Islam's sacred text.

It was far-fetched and unwarranted to draw forth from the Qur'an blanket condemnation of the modern world as immoral and unjust. Qutb did this in condemning all things secular and modern in the *Milestones* as "jahili" (Qutb's terminology meaning "ignorant", hence "unlawful"). For Qutb—as it was for Hasan al-

Banna, Maududi, Khomeini, *et al*—the renewal of Islam meant an open declaration of *jihād* against the secular modern world as corrupt, impure, and lacking in the worship of God. Qutb wrote in *Milestones*,

> If we look at the sources and foundations of modern ways of living, it becomes clear that the whole world is steeped in **Jahiliyyah** [meaning ignorance of the Divine guidance], and all the marvelous material comforts and high-level inventions do not diminish this ignorance. This **Jahiliyyah** is based on rebellion against God's sovereignty on earth. It transfers to man one of the greatest attributes of God, namely sovereignty, and makes some men lords over others. It is now not in that simple and primitive form of the ancient **Jahiliyyah**, but takes the form of claiming that the right to create values, to legislate rules of collective behavior, and to choose any way of life rests with men, without regard to what God has prescribed (emphasis, or bold letters, given in the translated text).[27]

Such Qutbian gibberish, or Ibn Taymiyya's recycled bigotry of pronouncing *takfīr* (anathema) on anyone who disagreed with him, was sermonized in mosques and circulated in pamphlets and on the Internet by Muslim fundamentalists in repudiating Muslim modernizers. And just as the gibberish of Mao Zedong in the *Red Book* mobilized Chinese youths in the massively bloody and destructive Cultural Revolution (1966-76), the gibberish of Qutb, Khomeini, Maududi and other Islamist ideologues schooled the ranks of unemployed and under-employed lumpen youths of the Muslim world to take arms against the forces of the modern world in their midst.

It was not merely the centuries separating Sayyid Qutb from Ghazali, it was how distant and lowly was Qutb's place in comparison to the place at the summit of jurisprudence and metaphysical discourse that Ghazali had occupied. Eric Ormsby in *Ghazali: The Revival of Islam* noted Ghazali "deserves to be counted among the great figures in intellectual history, worthy to be ranked with Augustine and Maimonides, Pascal and Kierkegaard."[28]

In what is generally considered by most historians and scholars of Islam (Muslims and non-Muslims) to be Ghazali's masterwork in several volumes, *Ihya' 'ulum al-din*, or "The Revival of the Religious Sciences", the much revered Muslim sage dwelled on a vast corpus of subjects from the "fundamentals" of religion to "table manners." The *Ihya'* was a summing up by Ghazali of his life's experience on how to orient oneself on the path of knowledge and devotion to truth, which was the truer and more sublime meaning of *jihād* as the "struggle within oneself" in quest of God. This meaning of *jihād*, according to Sufis among whom Ghazali had sought his own spiritual enlightenment, is as distant from the debasement of *jihād's* meaning by Sayyid Qutb as is the distance in the meaning of "love" from that of "rape."

Ghazali meant by the revival of Islam, even as the world around him fragmented, the awakening of Muslims as believers (*mo'min*) to man's destiny that the Qur'an alludes to in the allegory of the Prophet's "night journey". There could be no renewal of Islam for Ghazali without awakening within man the awareness of how precariously he is situated in Pascalian term between the beast and the angel inside of him, as Ormsby indicated, and who takes God's revelation as the "rope" to raise himself to the heights of his better nature.

In *Ihya'* Ghazali described man as one who "drops at one time to the lowest of the low and sinks to the level of demons and yet, how it rises at other times to the highest of the high and ascends to the realm of the angels who bask in God's nearness."[29] Divine revelation, Ghazali explained, was about liberating fallen and bewildered man trapped in conflicts of his own making and in showing him the path back to his origin. The intellectual orphans of Ghazali, from Ibn Taymiyya to Sayyid Qutb, deliberately misread the Qur'an and confounded by their own fanaticism slid downwards into the company of "the lowest of the low."

xiii.

The Qur'an problem—of how to read and comprehend God's Word—remains at the core of the struggle among Muslims and within Islam. The very first word of revelation to Muhammad was the command *Iqra* ("Read"). But then, "read" what?

"Read" was the Spoken Word to Muhammad. It was both a command and an invitation for man to gaze upon the universe, to metaphorically read it as a text, and then to reflect upon the nature of the Author given the immensity of His power on display. The Qur'an proclaims:

> Blessed be He in whose hand is the Kingdom—
> He is powerful over everything—
> who created death and life, that He might try you
> which of you is fairest in works; and He is
> the All-mighty, the All-forgiving—
> who created seven heavens one upon another.
> Thou seest not in the creation
> of the All-merciful any imperfection.
> Return thy gaze; seest thou any fissure?
> Then return thy gaze again, and again, and thy gaze comes
> back to thee dazzled, aweary (57:1-5).

The Qur'an is not a book of physics, astronomy, medicine, or science of any sort; the Qur'an is also not a book of history, a biography of prophets, or a manual of jurisprudence. It is *revelation* by which God reveals Himself to people, or to those among people, Muslims, who take the revelation as a matter of belief to be God's Word. Those who do, for them the Qur'an is moral guidance to travel the "straight path" toward God. And for them, for Muslims, the Qur'an describes itself in the opening verses of the second *Surah* (Chapter):

> This is the Book, wherein is no doubt,
> a guidance to the godfearing
> who believe in the Unseen, and perform the prayer,
> and expend of that We have provided them;

who believe in what has been sent down before thee,
and have faith in the Hereafter;
those are upon guidance from their Lord,
those are the ones who prosper (2:1-4).

After a lifetime spent in the study of scriptures and as professor of comparative religion, Wilfrid Cantwell Smith summed up his reflections on the Qur'an to write,

> For Muslims, the Qur'an has been received as the *ipsissima verba* of God Himself: God speaking to humankind not merely in seventh-century Arabia to Muhammad, but from all eternity to every man and woman throughout the world—including individual Muslim as he or she reads or recites it or devoutly holds it, or vividly or dimly or even unconsciously remembers a passage or phrase from it. It represents the eternal breaking through into time; the unknowable disclosed; the transcendent entering history and remaining here, available to mortals to handle and to appropriate; the divine become apparent.[30]

And therein lies the *Qur'an problem*, since how it is read, understood, and inspires individuals, groups, clans, tribes, and nations to conduct their affairs will vary as it has ever since Muhammad—the "walking Qur'an" in his wife Ayesha's description—departed from this world. The Qur'an will continue to be read differently, and a chasm will separate those of shallow minds and hearts veiled in ignorance from those who discern the splendor of truth and are drawn toward God as moths to flame. The former are the "children of darkness" who spread disorder, and containing them will always be a test for the "children of light."

Ghazali's journey into the "other Islam" and experience of living with Sufis brought for him the disclosure that human souls are ranked by the mystics of Islam according to the degree of ignorance, or darkness, which veils their hearts. Consequently, the Everlasting Light illumes hearts to the extent individuals have persevered during their life's journey in removing veils covering them in varying degrees of darkness. In *Mishkat* Ghazali noted the characteristics of those people he described as "veiled by pure darkness", and among them he mentioned there were Muslims. He wrote,

> There is one class which has thought that this world's Chief End is the satisfaction of one's wants, lusts, and animal pleasures, whether connected with sex, or food, or drink, or raiment. These, therefore, are the creatures of pleasure; pleasure is their god, the goal of their ambition, and in winning her they believe that they have won felicity. Deliberately and willingly do they place themselves at the level of beasts of the field; nay, at a viler level than the beasts. Can darkness be conceived more intense than this? Such men are, indeed, veiled by darkness unadulterated. Another class has thought that man's Chief End is conquest and domination—the taking of prisoners, and captives, and life. Such is the idea of the Arabs, certain of the Kurds, and withal very numerous fools. Their veil is the dark veil of the ferocious attributes, because these dominate them, so that they deem the running down of their quarry the height of bliss. These, then, are content to occupy the level of beasts of prey, ay, one more degraded still.[31]

The class of Muslims driven by, or preoccupied with, "conquest and domination" of others were in Ghazali's time, as they remain at present, adherents of political Islam. Their hearts are "veiled by pure darkness" even as they publicly profess faith, recite the Qur'an, raise and wave the banner of Islam, and insist on restoring the Caliphate while enforcing Shariah. They are the "children of darkness" and agents of disorder in the world.

The antithesis of political Islam is the "other Islam" experienced and lived by those whom Ghazali discovered after his mid-life crisis. Between the two is spread the entire spectrum of reading, recitation, memorization, and exegesis of the Qur'an. The test of which reading is most righteous and illuminating is one that helps guide a Muslim on the right path and places him in the company of those with the best conduct consistent with the "golden rule." And such reading occurs, as Ghazali might have said, when that Muslim's heart luminously radiates the two most precious attributes or names—the Ever Merciful (*ar-Rahman*) and the Compassionate (*ar-Rahim*)—by which God reveals Himself in the Qur'an.

V.

Arab and Muslim AntiSemitism

In Islamic society hostility to the Jew is non-theological.

Bernard Lewis[1]

Islam saved Jewry. This is an unpopular, discomforting claim in the modern world. But it is a historical truth. The argument for it is double. First, in 570 CE, when the Prophet Mohammad was born, the Jews and Judaism were on the way to oblivion. And second, the coming of Islam saved them, providing a new context in which they not only survived, but flourished, laying foundations for subsequent Jewish cultural prosperity – also in Christendom – through the medieval period into the modern world.

David J. Wasserstein[2]

The contemporary resurgence of post-*Shoah* anti-Semitism in Europe is an indisputable and menacing reality.[3] It is also an indisputable and menacing reality that the resurgent anti-Semitism in Europe rides, or is fuelled by, the even more menacing spread of Arab and Muslim anti-Semitism globally. Muslim anti-Semitism is driven by anti-Jew and anti-Israeli hatred packaged as religiously sanctioned by Muslim clerics such as Sheikh Yusuf al-Qaradawi, the Qatari-based leader of the Muslim Brotherhood from Egypt, and the clerical based political leadership of the Islamic Republic in Iran. Hence, the moot question in discussing Muslim anti-Semitism is in finding to what extent it is traceable to or rooted in the Qur'an and in the life of Muhammad, and to what extent it is a modern phenomenon that is in part imported from the West and in part a symptom of the deep-seated crisis of civilization within the Muslim world.

It is important, I believe, to examine forthrightly whether the Qur'an and the *Sira* (the biographical literature on the Prophet) sanction Islamic bigotry towards Jews or not for the following reasons. First, if Muslim anti-Semitism is religiously based then it can be said there is no reprieve from the cycle of Islamic Judeophobia and that a future catastrophe for Jews and Muslims might only be postponed, but may not be averted. Secondly, it then follows any relationship with Israel and Israelis based on mutual respect and interest, as sought by the late President Anwar Sadat of Egypt, is mistaken from Muslim perspective and contrary to the traditionally scripted relationship instituted in the early years of Islamic history in which Jews were accorded the status of *dhimmi* or protected people subordinate to the status of Muslims. And thirdly, opposition to Muslim anti-Semitism by Jews, Christians, other non-Muslims, and even by Muslims, invariably leads to a conflict with more or less the entirety of Islam.

I approach this subject from the perspective that Arab and Muslim anti-Semitism is a modern phenomenon, and attempts by Muslims to give legitimacy to this politics and culture of hate by citing the Qur'an or the traditions of the Prophet as references are not merely misguided but constitute an abuse of Islam and its sacred texts. When non-Muslims, particularly Jews for understandable reasons, give credence to the thesis of Muslim hate-mongers that their derogatory views about Jews are derived from the Qur'an and the biography of the Prophet, then they are paradoxically legitimating Muslim anti-Semitism with potentially lethal consequences for Israel. It is also ominous that in the early decades of the twenty-first century Israel found itself in the middle of the raging conflicts of the Middle East that are in origin tribal and sectarian and whose causes are internal to the fractious and schismatic nature of Arab-Muslim history; and even though Israel has no role nor bear any responsibility for these conflicts yet it cannot insulate itself from their effects.

I believe that in confronting Muslim hate-mongers and anti-Semites, the paramount urgency is to deny and de-legitimize their abusive reading of Islam's sacred texts. Indeed, the quelling of

Muslim hate-mongers is inseparable from advancing modernist reform of Islam, and this is why non-Muslims are mistaken when they make allowance for the thesis of Arab and Muslim anti-Semites, or agree with them, that Islam obliges Muslims to fight Jews as enemies of Allah.

Robert Wistrich rightly identified Muslim anti-Semitism as "a clear and present danger."[4] He painstakingly described the vile characterizations of Jews by Muslims; and those most depraved in spewing their bigotry against Jews are Palestinian Arabs and their religious, political and intellectual leaders.[5] The role of Haj Amin al-Husseini, the Mufti of Jerusalem, as Hitler's collaborator in importing European anti-Semitism into the Middle East is well documented.[6] The Mufti's ideology and politics has not been disavowed openly and in public by Palestinians, or by religious and political leaders among Arabs or Muslims in general. To the contrary, the Mufti's ideology of hate-mongering against Jews and the Zionist project has been emulated by an array of other leading Arab and Muslim intellectuals, activists, and religious leaders including Hasan al-Banna, the founder of the Muslim Brotherhood; Sayyid Qutb, the intellectual heavyweight of the Muslim Brothers; Sheikh Ahmed Yassin, the founder of Hamas; the rulers, religious leaders and imams of Saudi Arabia; the clerics of al-Azhar, the most renowned and prestigious Sunni Muslim religious institution, in Cairo, Egypt; Abul A'la Maududi, the Indo-Pakistani founder of the Jamaat-i-Islami; Ayatollah Khomeini, the Iranian architect of the Islamic Republic with its current Supreme Leader Ayatollah Ali Khamenei and, notably, the former presidents Akbar Rafsanjani and Mahmoud Ahmedinejad; the leaders of Hizbullah in Lebanon; Sheikh Yusuf al-Qaradawi, the popular Egyptian cleric on al-Jazeerah television network based in Qatar; the leadership and ranks of al Qaeda and other "jihadi" (holy war) organizations, such as the Taliban in Afghanistan and Pakistan; and non-clerical or secular Muslim leaders like Mahathir Mohamad, the former prime minister of Malaysia. Clearly, the front of Muslim anti-Semitism is wide and deep.

It might be supposed that so many prominent Muslims cannot all be wrong in insisting that Islam sanctions their hatred for Jews, Zionists and Israel. History, however, is replete with examples of people proven wrong in their beliefs and politics, and eventually confronted with the consequences of their errors. In this regard, Islamic history itself bears testimony to the wrongs done by Muslims and for which they have suffered grievously.

ii.

The Jew-Muslim relationship, as the record from the earliest years of Islam shows, has been difficult and marked with quarrels that turned ugly. Muhammad's engagement with the Jews of Arabia, of those settled in Yathrib (later to be known as *Madinat-un-Nabi*, the Prophet's city or simply Medina once the Prophet permanently settled there) turned uneasy and culminated in the expulsion and reputed massacre of Jews. There are references to these events in the Qur'an and in the earliest biography of the Prophet. We are nevertheless compelled to ask if these references can be construed as evidence of Islam's "Ur-anti-Semitism" that Muslim hate-mongers deploy in sanctifying their vilification of Jews. According to Neil Kressel,

> The problem goes way beyond the Nazi-like rants of extremist clerics. And far from being a by-product of the Arab-Israeli conflict, Jew hatred has roots in the long history and complex theology of Islam.[7]

In elaborating his thesis Kressel points to Sheikh Mohamed Sayyid Tantawi, the former Grand Imam and Rector of the al-Azhar who died in 2010, as an example of a contemporary Muslim anti-Semite who validated his bigotry by appeal to traditional Muslim Judeophobia based on negative references to Jews in the Qur'an and in the traditions of the Prophet. Tantawi was viewed by many as a liberal Muslim reformer, and from his position of influence and authority he condemned suicide-bombings after September 11, 2001, defended the Egyptian-Israeli peace treaty signed by President Anwar Sadat and Prime Minister Menachem Begin, denounced female circumcision common in Egypt, supported the ban on niqab (the full face cover worn by some Muslim women), and promoted inter-faith meetings with Christian and Jewish religious leaders. But when it came to Jews and Israel Tantawi displayed anti-Semitism masked as traditional Muslim Judeophobia prevalent across the Muslim world. Kressel writes,

> His [Tantawi's] doctoral dissertation, written in 1969, disparaged Jews with an abundance of quotations from the Quran and other religious sources. In this lengthy theological work, he detailed the Jews' supposedly evil ways and how they purportedly endeavored to entrap the Muslims during Muhammad's era. Tantawi's reading of the Quran ascribes to the Jews a slew of unflattering characteristics, including wanton envy, lasciviousness, religious fanaticism, murderousness, and a tendency toward "semantic bickering." Jews, collectively, are accused of corrupting Allah's word, consuming the people's wealth, and most ominously, murdering Allah's prophets.[8]

And Kressel then observes, "Even if one assumes that the Quranic text offers some basis for Tantawi's inferences, a true religious moderate might have argued that the verses in question apply only to particular Jews living in Muhammad's day."[9] Tantawi did not; instead in a sermon delivered in April 2002 he called out Jews as "the enemies of Allah, descendants of apes and pigs."[10] This phrase refers to a verse in the Qur'an (2:65), and it is commonly deployed by Muslim hate-mongers against Jews and Israelis.

The depiction of Jews as loathsome by Tantawi, or Khomeini[11], or Sayyid Qutb is done, as Wistrich wrote, "not simply to morally delegitimize Israel as a Jewish state and a national identity in the Middle East, but to dehumanize Judaism and the Jewish people as such."[12] Such depiction with reference to the Qur'an and early Muslim history is, according to Bassam Tibi, the Islamization of European anti-Semitism.[13] And this could occur, in Tibi's view, because Judeophobia is present in Islamic history just as it is found in European history. But genocidal anti-Semitism, according to Tibi, is "a specifically European, primarily German, disease that never existed in Islam before the twentieth century."[14] Similarly, Wistrich observed,

> The persistence, integrity, and depth of this hatred should not blind us, however, to the fact that, historically speaking, anti-Semitism is a relatively new phenomenon in Arab culture and among Muslims in general. It did not exist as a significant force in the traditional Islamic world, although, as we shall see, some of the seeds of contemporary anti-Jewish attitudes can be found in the Koran and other early Islamic sources.[15]

There is a distinction to be made, as is done by Tibi and Wistrich, between pre-modern Judeophobia in general and modern anti-Semitism that arose in Europe, specifically in Germany. Antagonism toward Jews among Christians and Muslims in the pre-modern world was common, and both Christians and Muslims took recourse to their faith-traditions as warrant for their Judeophobia. But despite this commonality Christians and Muslims historically have differed in their relationship with Jews. According to Bernard Lewis,

> The story of a golden age of complete equality is, of course, nonsense. No such thing was possible or even conceivable. Indeed, among Christians and Muslims alike, giving equal rights or, more precisely, equal opportunities to unbelievers would have been seen not as a merit but as a dereliction of duty. But until fairly modern times there was a much higher degree of tolerance in most of the Islamic lands than prevailed in the Christian world. For centuries, in most of Europe Christians were very busy persecuting each other; in their spare time, they were persecuting Jews and expelling Muslims — all at a time when, in the Ottoman Empire and some other Islamic states,

> Jews and several varieties of Christians were living side by side fairly freely and comfortably.[16]

The fusion of traditional Muslim Judeophobia and European anti-Semitism occurred in the shadow of Nazi Germany with the import of the entire corpus of Russian and German anti-Semitism, from the fabricated *Protocols of the Elders of Zion* to the support for Hitler's policy of extermination of Jews, into the Middle East. This was the period during the inter-war years when the victors of World War I were precariously positioned in the Middle East as the Mandatory powers in the terminology of the League of Nations, while the former subject peoples of the Ottoman Empire restlessly aspired for their own independence and statehood.

The collapse of the Ottoman Empire brought political instability in that part of the Arab-Muslim world ruled directly by, or under the nominal authority of, the Ottoman Caliph-Sultan residing in Istanbul. And when in 1924 Mustapha Kemal and his supporters abolished the Caliphate and re-constituted the post-Ottoman Turkey as a modern republican state, an entirely new problem arose for Muslims. The issue of legitimate order was at the heart of the dispute that had broken out among the companions of the Prophet following his death, and what emerged through the ensuing discord was the institution of the Caliphate. The abolition of Caliphate by the Turkish leader meant Muslims were faced with the question of not only how to acquire independence eventually from European colonial rule, but also how to reach a consensus in respect to the nature of legitimate authority in the new and unsettled age of post-Caliphate Islam. The argument over restoration of the Caliphate in some form or other, or the creation of a Shariah-based Islamic state as its approximation, became the distinguishing feature of political Islam, or Islamism, the ideology of socio-political movements such as the Muslim Brotherhood.

The Muslim distress spread over the long period of decline of Islamic rule and loss of lands to European powers turned increasingly bitter, especially among Arabs, in the twentieth century following the partition of Palestine, the establishment of Israel, and the repeated defeats suffered by Arabs in their wars against Jews. Arabs and Muslims view this history as insufferable and as deeply humiliating—bitter feelings that find expression in the vilest denunciation of Jews as enemies of Islam and Muslims. Lewis wrote,

> Why then this special anger in the Muslim response to the end of Palestine and the birth of Israel? Part of this is certainly due to its position, in the very center of the Arab core of the Islamic world, and to its inclusion of the city of Jerusalem, which—after long and sometimes bitter disputes—was finally recognized as the third Holy City of Islam after Mecca and Medina. But most of all, the sense of outrage, as is clearly shown in countless speeches and writings, was aroused by the identity of those who inflicted these dramatic defeats on Muslim and Arab armies and imposed their rule on Muslim Arab populations. The victors were not the followers of a world religion or the armies of a mighty imperial power, by which one could be conquered without undue shame—not the Catholic kings of Spain, not the far-flung British Empire, not the immense and ruthless might of Russia—but the Jews, few, scattered, and powerless, whose previous humility made their triumphs especially humiliating.[17]

This recent history explains in part the nature of Arab and Muslim anti-Semitism, and why it continues to be ratcheted up in inverse relation to the repeated failures of Arabs to defeat Israel. It is also aggravated by the continuing discord over the nature of Islamic society, by the general economic, political and cultural malaise across the Muslim world, by the discrediting of secular-nationalist regimes, and by sectarian conflicts that have spilled over into civil war across the Middle East and beyond into the wider Muslim world. The unwillingness to examine the causes internal to Muslim culture and history for this civilizational crisis has fostered among Muslims a culture of denial, and a pathological proclivity to blame others, especially Jews.

While Arab and Muslim anti-Semitism might be explained as symptomatic of Islamic civilization in disarray, what is not explained and, I submit, cannot be explained is Muslim bigotry against Jews on the basis of Islam. If the argument that the Qur'an and the Prophet sanction Muslim Judeophobia is true as Muslim hate-mongers insist, then what logically follows is unavoidable. Just as few drops of lemon curdle a bowl of milk, Judeophobia sanctioned by the Qur'an and the Prophet would mean that Islam as a religion of mercy is a falsehood. As a Muslim I recoil at this thought as should any Muslim reflecting upon the fallacy of the argument that those few references in the Qur'an about some Jews, or a segment of the Jewish population with whom Muhammad had a bitter encounter, can be read, as Muslim hate-mongers do, as divine wrath directed toward all Jews till the end of time, and that it is incumbent upon Muslims to fight them as enemies of God. Such a reading of the Qur'an is plainly wrong and indefensible; the question, therefore, arises how the Qur'anic references to Jews should be read consistent with the overall message of the Qur'an that Muslims believe is a sign of God's mercy for mankind.

The Qur'an is also the testimony and record of Muhammad's life. The few biographical references to Muhammad in the Qur'an are what we indisputably know about him. These references constitute the core narrative or the bare outline of a life that was later much embroidered and embellished with imaginative writings of his biographers who assembled volumes of oral reports about the Prophet, most of them unreliable or of dubious merit, as supporting evidence of their scholarship. If Shakespeare's life remains contested despite the proximity of his age to ours, it is of no surprise that what we know of the Prophet with any degree of certainty is very little given the distance in time and, especially, since the people among whom he was born, the Arabs of the desert, lived at the margin of existing civilizations with scarce any mention in recorded history.[18] But it might also be said that since the Qur'an is the most authentic source of the little we know about the Prophet, the Qur'an vouchsafes the truthfulness of his life; it is a matter of Muslim belief that the Prophet conducted his affairs and lived his life consistent with the directives given to him as revealed in the Qur'an.

iii.

Islam was not a new religion that erupted in the relative barren soil of Arabia among a people at the margin of civilizations. It was instead the primordial faith in God of man—the faith first narrated in the Hebrew Bible—renewed at an inflection point in history that proved providentially immensely successful, as it seized the imagination and devotion of a people, the Arabs of the desert, and propelled them forward into the world as a new force bearing the old message of monotheism. The manner in which events surrounding this history unfolded was so remarkable that the shockwaves from that moment in the early decades of the seventh century of the Christian era still resonate more than fourteen centuries later.

In *Moses and Monotheism* Sigmund Freud speculated about Moses's life and origin. This was the last book he published in 1939 before his death, and in it he described Judaism as a Father religion and Christianity as a Son religion. This description of Judaism and Christianity is striking, and following Freud we might describe Islam as a return to the Father religion that, as Judaism, had evolved into a strict and uncompromising monotheism relative to the Christian belief in which the idea of One God was somewhat diluted due to the Greek-Roman influence. Though an atheist till the end, Freud's last work as a testimony of a thinker deeply influenced by the religion and culture of his Jewish ancestors was packed with striking insights and was written while he witnessed Europe sink into a new age of barbarism. Freud made one passing reference to Islam. He wrote,

> the founding of the Mohammedan religion seems to me to be an abbreviated repetition of the Jewish one, in imitation of which it made its appearance. There is reason to believe that the Prophet originally intended to accept the Jewish religion in full for himself and his people. The regaining of the one great primeval Father produced in the Arabs an extraordinary advance in self-confidence which led them to great worldly successes, but which, it is true, exhausted itself in these.[19]

Freud was not a scholar of Islam and though there is no indication given by his biographers that he ventured into any serious study of Islam and Arabs, it would not be unlikely that he had heard of, or come across, the writings of those Jewish scholars—for instance, Rabbi Abraham Geiger (1810-74) or Freud's contemporary, Ignaz Goldziher (1850-1921)—who made significant contributions in the study of Islam and its sacred texts, the Qur'an and the traditions of the Prophet. But Freud's remark quoted above echoed a theme advanced by Geiger in his prize-winning monograph of 1833, the title of which rendered into English was "What Did Muhammad Take From Judaism?"[20]

The thesis, according to Geiger, that "Muhammad in his Qur'an has borrowed much from Judaism as it presented itself to him in his time,"[21] is not strange given the numerous references to Hebrew prophets, their stories, and the highly elevated place Moses occupies in the Qur'an. Indeed, it might be said, the Qur'an is very much a Jewish text as much as Jews were not merely a "people of the Book" (*ahl al-Kitab*), but the *first* people in the Semitic tradition called upon to worship the one and only God. The religion of Jews and their stories were familiar to the pagan Arabs, for Jews had lived in Arabia for nearly a millennium before Muhammad's time.[22] And since Muhammad preached the message of worshipping one God, the God of Abraham, it was only natural and proper that he held up Jews, the Arabs' most proximate neighbours, as an example of a people subscribing to a monotheistic faith.

But the pagan Arabs, despite the length of time Jews had lived among them did not embrace the Jewish faith, nor did they accept Christianity with which they were also familiar. It took revelation from God to a man born among them, belonging to them by blood and customs, to wrench them away from polytheism and embrace the idea of one God, *Allah* in Arabic.

Muslims believe that Muhammad did not borrow from Judaism or Christianity, but preached the message revealed to him and which message originating from the same source Jews and Christians hold as true. There is one truth revealed successively under different circumstances to different people at different places, according to Muslim belief, and what was revealed to Muhammad was that one eternal truth in the circumstances of the time and place in which his divinely ordained mission occurred.

God's revelation to Muhammad is the Qur'an, and for Muslims the Qur'an is as matter of belief God's Word. Frithjof Schuon (1907-98), a philosopher, poet, and teacher of the "perennial philosophy" of German origin wrote,

> The great theophany of Islam is the Quran; it presents itself as being a "discernment" (*furqan*) between truth and error.[23]

Before there was a text compiled of the revelations given to Muhammad, there was only the Word of God as he heard and it was through him that others received the Word. The Qur'an describes itself as revelation that "makes things clear" (15:1). Nevertheless, it is difficult to grasp the full meaning of divine texts like the Qur'an given the nature of the language that is frequently allusive and elliptical. The same is true for the Bible. According to Schuon,

> The seeming incoherence of these texts—for instance the Song of Songs or certain passages of the Pauline Epistles—always has

> the same cause, namely the incommensurable disproportion between the Spirit on the one hand and the limited resources of human language on the other: it is as though the poor and coagulated language of mortal man would break under the formidable pressure of the Heavenly Word into a thousand fragments, or as if God, in order to express a thousand truths, had but a dozen words at his disposal and so was compelled to make use of allusions heavy with meaning, of ellipses, abridgements and symbolic syntheses. A sacred Scripture—and let us not forget that for Christianity Scripture includes not only the Gospels but the whole Bible with all its enigmas and seeming scandals—is a totality, a diversified image of Being, diversified and transfigured for the sake of the human receptacle; it is a light that wills to make itself visible to clay, or wills to take the form of that clay; or still in other words, it is a truth which, since it must address itself to beings compounded of clay, has no means of expression other than the very substance of the nescience of which our soul is made.[24]

Hence, how to read the Qur'an—how to distinguish between what is the universal and timeless truth embedded in the particular, how to go beyond the explicit (*zähir*) statements and grasp or discover the implicit or hidden (*bätin*) meaning of the text, how not to misuse and abuse the allegorical language of the Qur'an for partisan purposes—has been contentious ever since the Prophet's demise. From the earliest discord that ruptured the community of believers Muhammad left behind, the sectarian conflicts which eventually led to the massacre of his family, the proliferation of sects among Muslims, the tribal wars fought in the name of Islam, to the raging conflicts across the Arab-Muslim world in our time, the history of the House of Islam reflects abiding disagreements among Muslims over how the Qur'an is read—differences in the sacred text of Islam that all too frequently erupted in violence. Islam's success in history ironically exacerbated the differences among its followers; politics inevitably corrupted faith when pagan Arabs, as recently converted Muslims, carved out a vast empire and their tribal chiefs emerged as imperial rulers in the manner of the Byzantine and Persian oriental despots.

But differences among Muslims, especially among the religious scholars, the *ulema*, also stimulated the variety and richness of Muslim learning during the expansive phase of the Islamic civilization in the first half millennium of Muslim history. The innumerable commentaries on the Qur'an produced in this period were indicative of the need to make non-Arab Muslims familiar with the language of the sacred text they were required to learn and to comprehend what they were reading. Yet regardless of how the text was read, the one incontrovertible fact was that though the Qur'an was revealed in a world filled with strife, it taught man could find the path to peace and tranquillity provided he faithfully bore witness to one God and took His message to heart. The Qur'an warns, reminds, explains and provides lessons from history, but it is not vindictive, because God, as the Qur'an repeatedly affirms, is ever merciful. Hence, the alleged seeds of contemporary anti-Jewish attitudes found in the Qur'an should be read figuratively and contextually, as these were understood when revealed to the Prophet, and lessons learned from what follows when any people, in this case some among Jews, squandered the trust placed in them by the God of Abraham and Moses. Moreover, references in the Qur'an to those Jews of Medina—for example, the Jews of Banu Qurayza—or of Arabia, who opposed the Prophet and lent support to his enemies, are specifically directed at them and not directed toward *all* Jews as people of the Book. Those Jews, the opponents of the Prophet, are referred to with the article "the"—in Arabic *al*—as in "the Jews" and identified in particular as such; the mention in the Qur'an of "the Jews" must not be taken as reference to Jews in general. In referring to the Arabic article *al*, or the article "the" in English, Dr. Tawfik Hamid, an Egyptian-American, writes,

> "The" is a definite article that refers to something specific. When "the" is absent, the object of a statement is universal; when it is present, it refers to a specific subset of a collection... A Muslim...instructed all along to heed "al" strictly in its historical context...would no longer be permitted to kill nonbelievers...
>
> It is amazing that this vital emphasis on the word "the"—an emphasis that can mean the difference between life and death—is not available in any approved *tafsir* [commentary] of the Quran.[25]

The few negative references to Jews in the Qur'an describe how a segment among them residing in Arabia mounted opposition against Muhammad, and how he responded. The Jewish opposition located in Medina turned into collusion with the Meccan enemies of the Prophet, as in the indictment and punishment of the Jews of Banu Qurayza. If this collusion had succeeded it would have meant defeat, death, and the end of Muhammad's divinely ordained mission. These references are to particular events; they are elliptical, and they bear universal lessons. Moreover, those Jews specifically addressed in the Qur'an—the Jews in the time of Muhammad who opposed him—understood the allusions made in these verses to their own sacred text.

The Qur'anic admonishment, "Be ye apes, despised and rejected," and hurled by Muslim hate-mongers at Jews is found in the verse that reads in Muhammad Asad's translation as follows:

> [F]or you are well aware of those from among you who profaned the Sabbath, whereupon we said unto them, "Be as apes despicable!" – and set them up as a warning example for their time and for all times to come, as well as an admonition to all who are conscious of God (2:65-66).

The admonishment is figurative. There is reference here to the Mosaic Law, which condemns Jews violating the Sabbath with death as punishment according to the Hebrew Scripture.[26] These words came as a warning to the Jews opposing Muhammad, and as a reminder of what befell those who departed from the right path after God had shown mercy to them—a lesson also emphasized in preceding verses of the Qur'an. Verse 2:62, the most significant in this section—the second and the longest chapter in the Qur'an called "Al-Baqarah" (The Cow)—states in Asad's translation:

> Verily, those who have attained to faith [in this divine writ], as well as those who follow the Jewish faith, and the Christians, and the Sabians–all who believe in God and the Last Day and do righteous deeds–shall have their reward with their Sustainer; and no fear need they have, and neither shall they grieve (2:62).

In his commentary on this verse Asad wrote,

> The above passage–which recurs in the Qur'an several times–lays down a fundamental doctrine of Islam. With a breadth of vision unparalleled in any other religious faith, the idea of "salvation" is here made conditional upon three elements only: belief in God, belief in the Day of Judgment, and righteous action in life.[27]

I refer to Asad's translation of the Qur'an and the accompanying commentary because he excelled in both languages, Arabic and English, and his personal history. Asad (1900-92), named Leopold Weiss at birth, was a Polish Jew and grandson of a rabbi. As an adult, Asad became a Muslim, lived in Saudi Arabia and later in Spain, and devoted his life to the study of the Qur'an and Islam.[28] In his prologue to *The Message of the Qur'an*, Asad wrote, "It is axiomatic from the Islamic perspective that the Qur'an cannot be translated, because the *form* of God's revelation, that is the Arabic itself, is not merely incidental to its meaning, but essential to it... A rendering into another language, therefore, is not and never can be the Qur'an as such, but merely an interpretation of it." Asad devoted his life to learning the Arabic of the Qur'an, or the closest living approximation to it spoken among those dwindling numbers of Bedouins of the Arabian Desert still not assimilated into the rapidly changing world around them by the reach of the "modernized" Arabic in radio and television broadcasts from the urban centres of the Arab world.

As Asad's commentary indicates, verse 2:62 bears the universal message of the Qur'an. It belies any justification of Muslim anti-Jewish bigotry; it nullifies any suggestion that Jews, as a result of opposition by some Jews against Muhammad, are condemned as enemies of God and the Prophet. The idea that the sins of one generation, or one individual, might be visited upon another is explicitly rejected in the Qur'an in the following words, "And no bearer of burdens shall be made to bear another's burden" (35:18). The ill will toward Jews in the pre-modern world could not be derived from the Qur'an. Nonetheless, many Muslims—followers of a faith-tradition that turned triumphantly imperial and yet was open and inviting to non-Muslims—viewed Jews negatively because, as Muslims, they could not understand why Jews as a people did not embrace Islam.

The story about the Jews of Banu Qurayza—their collusion with the Meccans, the resistance they offered after the pagan confederates were beaten, their surrender and their punishment—is referred to in the Qur'an briefly thus: "and He brought down from their strongholds those of the followers of earlier revelation who had aided the aggressors, and cast terror into their hearts; some you slew; and some you made captive" (33:26). Ibn Ishaq, the first biographer of the Prophet, writing some 145 years after the events relating to the Banu Qurayza, embroidered and embellished this brief reference in the Qur'an by gathering together oral reports of what presumably occurred. According to Ibn Ishaq's history, the men of Banu Qurayza were condemned to death by Sa'd b. Mu'adh, the arbitrator nominated by the Jews to decide their fate, and women and children sold into slavery. Ibn Ishaq reported that Muhammad carried out the verdict. The estimates for the men of Banu Qurayza killed by Muslims on that fateful day in Medina vary between 400 and 900. The validity of this story, the veracity of Ibn Ishaq, and the meaning of this event in relation to the Prophet and his teaching have all been disputed.[29]

From the present day perspective the judgment was harsh, but was it also harsh under the circumstances and customs of the time? Though the story of Banu Qurayza stands as a rebuke of the Prophet among his critics irrespective of any explanation offered, the explanation nevertheless is neither difficult nor anti-Jewish. As noted earlier, if the treachery of the Banu Qurayza in colluding with the pagan confederates led by the Meccan enemies of the Prophet had turned out as planned it would have likely spelled the end for the Prophet and Islam. The stakes were immensely high, and the leaders of Banu Qurayza were fully aware of this outcome if their plan had succeeded. It was also exceedingly ironic that the Jews of Banu Qurayza, a people of the Book and monotheists, colluded with polytheists against Muhammad preaching monotheism to pagan Arabs. From the point of view of the Qur'an it was providential that Muhammad prevailed, thereby teaching a timely lesson to those still maintaining their hostility to his message and mission. Moreover, the punishment meted out to the men of Banu Qurayza was not inconsistent with the tenets of the Hebrew Scripture. Here reference might be made to the judgment of Moses delivered when he came down from the Mount Sinai and saw his people, as if engaged in treason against God who had delivered them from their captivity in Egypt, worshipping a golden calf sculpted out of their jewellery. Moses called out upon his men, the Levites, and ordered them to draw their swords and slay the men who had done wrong, and some three thousand were put to death.[30]

Moses is the prophet of Jews, and since I referred to Freud's striking description of Judaism and Christianity I shall quote him here again. Freud wrote, "And since we know that behind the God who chose the Jews and delivered them from Egypt stood the man Moses, who achieved that deed, ostensibly at God's command, I venture to say this: it was one man, the man Moses, who created the Jews."[31] Moses is the towering presence in the Hebrew Scripture and, similarly, he is in the Qur'an. Muslims revere him and address him as "kalimullah," the one who spoke with God. The reference to Moses and the punishment he meted out to those responsible for making and worshipping an image is not inapt nor improper in discussing the penalty carried out against the Jewish men of Banu Qurayza, especially as Moses's draconian punishment of the idol worshippers would have been readily understood at the time by all involved in the events surrounding Banu Qurayza and the Prophet. Just as much of the traditional reports or *hadīth* literature about the Prophet is of dubious merit, the accounts of what occurred with the Jews of Banu Qurayza remain doubtful.

Regardless, if the story of Banu Qurayza was so egregious and out of proportion to the norms of the time, it would have reverberated beyond the confines of Arabia and been reported, or at least taken note of, in the contemporary chronicles recorded in Jewish and Christian centres of Byzantine and Persia. Yet there is no independent record of the story of Banu Qurayza found outside of Muslim sources beginning with Ibn Ishaq's first biography of the Prophet. The earliest notice of Islam in Christian records is found in the *History of Heraclius* prepared by the Armenian bishop Sebeos and completed around 661, less than thirty years after the death of Muhammad. In this account, Sebeos recorded that Jews sought assistance of Arabs in the defence of Edessa from the Byzantines. Sebeos also referred to the Arabs as the children of Ishmael, and he mentioned that Muhammad preached to the Arabs about the God of Abraham and the connection of Islam's origin with the Jewish faith. Sebeos made no mention of Banu Qurayza, or of any other event or matter related to Islam indicating Arab hostility to Jews. Instead, as John Moorhead noted, "Sebeos' evaluation of Islam was positive."[32] When the Arab armies conquered Palestine and captured Jerusalem—events that took place a few years after the Jews of

Banu Qurayza were punished—Jews celebrated the defeat of the Byzantines and saw the new rulers as a positive change for their own situation in the land of their ancestors. Such a receptive attitude by Jews toward Arabs would have been at best odd, even scandalously hypocritical, if they had known about Banu Qurayza and, as a result, nurtured enmity against Islam. Until Ibn Ishaq narrated this story and likely embellished it, as W.N. Arafat has indicated,[33] there was nothing about it except for the reference in the Qur'an that might have alarmed the people outside of Arabia. Yet there was no such alarm; and Jews, despite their long tradition of recording events that affected them for good or ill, of that period in history made no record of this alleged massacre of the Jews of Banu Qurayza. No independent credible account of this event, if it did occur, has surfaced apart from Arab sources written more than a century after the death of the Prophet.

We might ask if there is any lesson in these events as recorded in scriptures beyond the generic rule, that men are answerable for their deeds? For believers in God, history is providential. Yet even the prophets were liable to be mistaken sometimes and, therefore, accountable for their errors on the Day of Reckoning. Lesser men should not presume to act as divine agents. Consequently, since for Muslims revelation came to an end with Muhammad as the last of God's prophets, any Muslim claiming to emulate the Prophet or to act as if he has God's sanction is simply gross presumptuous and delusional.

It is this presumptuousness and delusion that fill the minds of the intemperate and self-described "jihadis" or "holy warriors" in the ranks of al Qaeda, Islamic State of Iraq and Syria (ISIS), Lashkar-e-Taiba, Hamas, Taliban, and others who selectively seize hold of verses from the Qur'an as sanction for their violence. This is not a new development, and it can be traced back to the earliest years of discord following the Prophet's demise that divided the community of believers. Islamists in recent years have prioritized Chapter 9 of the Qur'an—"At-Tawbah" or "Repentance"—as God's sanction to wage war on the infidels, including Jews and Christians. The verse invoked by Islamists, and variously known as the War Verse or the Sword Verse, reads as follows (in Asad's translation),

> [And] fight against those who—despite having been vouchsafed revelation [aforetime]—do not [truly] believe either in God or the Last Day, and do not consider forbidden that which God and His Apostle have forbidden, and do not follow the religion of truth [which God has enjoined upon them], till they [agree to] pay the exemption tax with a willing hand, after having been humbled [in war] (9: 29).

According to the Franco-Tunisian scholar Abdelwahab Meddeb, this verse was "invoked, for example, by the Armed Islamic Group (GIA) terrorists who massacred the monks of Tibhirine in Algeria in 1996. The same verse is said to grant religious legitimacy to the suicide bombers of Hamas in Israel. The same reference may well have been involved in galvanizing the criminals responsible for the horrifying attacks on September 11, 2001, in New York and Washington, D.C."[34]

There is little that can be done to prevent those Muslims and their hate-mongering teachers, such as Hasan al-Banna, Sayyid Qutb, Khomeini, Sheikh Yusuf al-Qaradawi or Mullah Omar who cite the Sword Verse, or some other similar verses, as an excuse to precipitate and justify violence. Violence begets violence, and we witnessed how Algeria, for example, descended into the nightmare of terrorist atrocities in the 1990s, when a brutal war between the state and the Islamists was fought. There are too many similar examples from recent Muslim history that might be mentioned. The point to be emphasized is that the traditional exegesis of Chapter 9, which contains the Sword Verse, was overwhelmingly one of caution. The revelation of Chapter 9 is from the Medina period of the Prophet's life, a period of warfare with the pagan confederacy in which segments of the Jewish population, such as members of the Banu Qurayza, colluded against Islam. In his commentary on Chapter 9 and, particularly, in reference to the Sword Verse, Asad noted, "it must be read in the context of the clear-cut Qur'anic rule that war is permitted only in self-defence."[35] Accordingly, we might state here that the wars Israel has fought since 1948 were mostly in self-defence and, therefore, consistent with the Qur'anic directives; if any of these wars that Israel fought against Arab states and terrorists ended in loss, it would have been an existential defeat for the Jewish state. Moreover, within the Muslim community, the authority responsible for initiating war in self-defence must also be legitimate, or seen to be legitimate by a majority of Muslims. Since the Prophetic era ended the arc of Muslim history has had to cope with a crisis of legitimacy. During the age of Islamic expansion in the early centuries of Islam, the Sword Verse was invoked to justify instituting the exemption tax or *jizya* on Jews and Christians living among Muslims, but that period of Muslim history ended a long time ago. In the post-Caliphate age, the historic religio-political challenge for Muslims lies in constructing the basis of a legitimate order consistent with democracy, freedom, human rights, gender equality, and science. The universal message of the Qur'an that would assist Muslims to meet this challenge is not found in the verses Muslim fanatics extol; it is found in those verses that these fanatics seek to deliberately downgrade in priority, or even go so far as to declare abrogated.

The Sudanese reformer Mahmoud Mohamed Taha contended Muslims had failed from the earliest years to comprehend the universal message of Islam. Taha was optimistic however and saw the modern age as a propitious time for Muslims to comprehend Islam's universality and accordingly reform the Shariah in keeping with the spirit of the modern age. Taha explained his reformist views in *The Second Message of Islam*, which got him into trouble with the authorities. His message was built around the proposition that there is a natural progression in Muslim understanding of the Qur'an that obligates the believers to evolve in their thinking so that they may eventually comprehend fully and better the universal message revealed to Muhammad. Taha was hanged by the regime headed by President Numeiri, the Sudanese dictator, in 1985.

The tragic fate of Taha illustrates the immense problems and the peril faced by modernist Muslim reformers. Reform of Islam means, in effect, either reforming the Shariah code—the corpus of Islamic laws derived from the Qur'an, the *hadīth* or traditions of the Prophet, and the *ijmā`* or consensus of the *ulema*—or setting it aside entirely and beginning afresh in the light of a modern legal-political philosophy, hermeneutics, comparative religion, theology, and cosmology. In Sunni Islam, to which the overwhelming majority of Muslims belong, Shariah is taken to be a fixed and inviolate legal system based on the accumulated wisdom, knowledge and consensus of the *ulema* from the classical period of Muslim history during the first three centuries of Islam. The need for independent reasoning or *ijtihād*, which scholars used to formulate Shariah, was declared closed by the consensus of Sunni *ulema* either in the twelfth century following the death of Al-Ghazali, the revered scholar-jurist turned mystic in 1111,[36] or, at the latest, in the thirteenth century following the sack of Baghdad by the Mongol armies in 1258. The Sunni leader, the Caliph of Islam, held, according to the consensus of the Sunni *ulema*, that there was no more need for *ijtihād* because there was nothing more to be added as new insights to the existing corpus of laws. Consequently, Muslim scholars were obligated to replace independent reasoning with *taqlīd* or imitation in the application of Shariah. As Robert Reilly has convincingly argued, this "closing of the Muslim mind" effectively doomed the pre-modern Islamic civilization once Europe emerged from its own relative state of backwardness into the making of the modern world.[37]

As Taha maintained, the prerequisite to the reform of Islam requires reading the Qur'an anew in keeping with the spirit of the age in which people live. Muslims revere the Qur'an as the Word of God, which is also their core doctrinal belief. Accordingly, it might be argued, the Qur'an cannot be a closed or frozen text with a fixed meaning determined by the dead weight of men from another time long past; in other words, the Qur'an addresses the believers in their time. This necessity of reading the Qur'an with fresh eyes and insight is threatening to the orthodoxy, the Islamists, the defenders of the status quo and Muslims in general who dread or disapprove of change and openness in closed societies. A reading of the Qur'an that relies only, as Islamists insist, on the explicit and literal meaning of the text will fail to comprehend the essential unity of the Qur'an's message due to the prevalence of apparent contradictions scattered across the text. It is only by openness to reading the Qur'an as a text with a hierarchy of implicit meanings that Muslims can be prepared to comprehend the universal message of the Qur'an and set it apart from the subsidiary meanings in the text.

In the surah/chapter "Al-Maa'idah" or "The Repast" (Chapter 5 in the Qur'an), we read, "O You who have attained to faith! Do not take the Jews and the Christians for your allies" (5: 51). Like the Sword Verse in Chapter 9, this is another favourite passage of Islamist and fundamentalist Muslims. It happens that "Al-Maa'idah" is one of the last chapters of the Qur'an revealed in Medina sometime after the Prophet's farewell pilgrimage a decade after the *hijra* (flight) from Mecca to Medina or in the tenth year of Islam. This chapter also contains the verse declaring: "Today have I perfected your religious law for you, and have bestowed upon you the full measure of My blessings, and willed that self-surrender unto Me [al-Islam] shall be your religion" (5: 3). And as we read further in "Al-Maa'idah", we come across the following verse, "[V]erily, those who have attained to faith [in this divine writ], as well as those who follow the Jewish faith, and the Sabians, and the Christians—all who believe in God and the Last Day and do righteous deeds—no fear need they have, and neither shall they grieve" (5: 69). Hence, what we have here in "Al-

Maa'idah" or Chapter 5, revealed after the Sword Verse found in "At-Tawbah" or Chapter 9, is a negative reference to Jews and Christians that is diluted or set aside by the universal message that is inclusive and stated clearly. According to Meddeb, "it is here that the ethical vocation becomes the criterion for salvation, beyond any consideration of belief in any so-called true religion."[38] It is here also, and even more importantly, that the universal message of the Qur'an nullifies the presumptuousness, or hubris, of fanatical monotheists (be they Muslims, Christians, or Jews) who insist their religion is the only true belief. And to emphasize this universal message so that there is no mistaking that ethical conduct is the measure of the quality of faith, the Qur'an informs in "Al-Maa'idah" that differences among faiths are not accidental:

> Unto every one of you have We appointed a [different] law and way of life. And if God had so willed, He could surely have made you all one single community: but [He willed it otherwise] in order to test you by means of what He has vouchsafed unto you. Vie, then, with one another in doing good works! Unto God you all must return; and then He will make you truly understand all that on which you were wont to differ (5:48).

Moreover, according to the methodology of traditional exegesis, the Sword Verse is abrogated by the relevant verses of "Al-Maa'idah." This principle of abrogation (*naskh*) was developed by early Muslim jurists as a remedy for *apparent* inconsistencies in the Qur'an by giving precedence to a verse revealed later over one revealed earlier. As Carl Ernst explains, the "harmonizing approach acknowledges a chronological dimension to the unfolding of the Qur'an, as is evident from the traditional labelling of suras as belonging to the earlier Meccan period or the later Medinan period."[39] While both "At-Tawbah" containing the Sword Verse and "Al-Maa'idah" were revealed in Medina, "Al-Maa'idah" was revealed in the final year of the Prophet's life and, consequently, takes precedence over "At-Tawbah." And while the idea of abrogation, according to Muhammad Asad, is faulty[40] and, according to Taha, it goes against the spirit of the Qur'an[41], it remains the methodology of traditionalism in Islamic jurisprudence, which, by its own reasoning, must conclude that the Sword Verse was abrogated by the universal message reiterated in "Al-Maa'idah."

Regardless, Islamist hate-mongers, such as Sheikh Yusuf al-Qaradawi, habitually insist upon the principle of abrogation when it serves their purpose and void it when it does not. Clearly, though, on the basis of traditional exegesis, there is no justification even in pre-modern times for anti-Jew bigotry among Muslims based on the Qur'anic references to Jews. Muslim Judeophobia since the earliest times has reflected the pathology of tribalism among Arabs and Muslims. In the continued justification of bigotry against Jews, Muslims wrongly cite the few negative references to them in the Qur'an that pertain to specific historical disputes between the Jews of Arabia and the Prophet and cannot be read as general condemnation of Jews as a people, as believers, and as the "people of the Book."

iv.

Violence is not specific or limited to Islam and Muslims. It is embedded in "the crooked timber of humanity"—a phrase of Immanuel Kant, which Sir Isaiah Berlin, the Anglo-Jewish philosopher, adopted as a motif of his work—that religion, ethics, moral philosophy, and education seek to remedy. On the basis of his psychoanalytic theory Freud explained that civilization is coercion writ large. The "replacement of the power of the individual by the power of a community," Freud wrote, "constitutes the decisive step of civilization."[42] Violence is contained, repressed, and re-directed as civilized life evolves. And, according to Freud, the grand project of civilization can only be realized, if at all, at some future date, when men shed their illusions and bring about a re-ordering of relations that makes coercion unnecessary and leads to its renunciation.[43]

Freud held that civilizations differ as a result of the specific history of each people and what recourse they have sought in striving for a legitimate and just socio-political order. Islamic history stands apart from that of Jews and Christians by the manner in which its founding drama and its success in emerging as a world power within the first century after Muhammad's death in 632 unfolded. Paradoxically the speed with which the frontiers of Islam spread fostered repression of the memory of the violence that surrounded it.

The Qur'an is filled with warnings in general about man's nature as given to forgetfulness and ingratitude, and his disposition to follow the instincts of his lower self. The warnings from the Hebrew Scripture about the reprobate characteristics of man reverberate in the Qur'an. But apart from the general nature of these warnings, there was also a specific warning to the Prophet to be wary of tribal Arabs when, after having been finally defeated in their campaigns against him and his followers, they came to swear allegiance in person to him. The relevant verse warns,

> The Bedouin say, "We have attained to faith."
> Say [unto them, O Muhammad]: You have not [yet] attained to faith; you should [rather] say, 'We have [outwardly] surrendered'—for [true] faith has not yet entered your hearts." (49: 14).

Beyond the immediacy of this warning to the Prophet, the verse also underscores the reality of hypocrites in society and the dangers they pose in causing harm around them.

The dispute over leadership of the Muslim community, or the Medinan state in embryo at the time of the Prophet's death, marked the beginning of the war within Islam. Those involved were companions of the Prophet, yet they displayed an insufficiency of belief or rightful conduct by their intemperate behaviour that ignited schismatic wars and violently severed the unity of the believers in Islam. The repressed memory of this blood-soaked history, has haunted Muslims from the earliest to the present time.[44]

Tribalism was deeply embedded among the first generation of Muslims and never fully renounced by the people among whom the Prophet was born and to whom he brought the message of Islam. Political power passed into the family of the Prophet's most ardent foe when Abu Sufyan's son Mu'awiya seized the Caliphate on the murder of Ali, the cousin and son-in-law of Muhammad. Mu'awiya founded the Ummayad dynasty based in Damascus, Syria, and his son Yazid approved of the action his men took against Hussein—the grandson of the Prophet through his only surviving daughter Fatima, married to Ali—when he asserted his claim to succeed his father as the Caliph. Hussein was brutally killed in Kerbala, Iraq, in 680, his body disfigured by horses made to trample over it, and his severed head carried at the point of a lance to the Caliph's palace in Damascus. In her account based on the earliest Muslim sources of the killing of Hussein and the great schism in Islam, Lesley Hazleton writes,

> As with the death of Christ, the death of Hussein soars beyond history into metahistory. It enters into the realm of faith and inspiration, of passion both emotional and religious.[45]

But Hussein's murder was much more; it was a crime of such proportion that Muslims buried their grief and shame within themselves even as they got divided. A minority among Muslims became partisans of the family of the Prophet through Fatima and her sons, Hasan and Hussein, and came to be known as Shi'a. The majority, known as Sunni, preferred to accept the authority of the Ummayad dynasty rather than further deepen the violent tribal discord, which had seized the rapidly growing Muslim community. In time the Sunni majority came to look down upon the

Shi'a minority with near contempt as responsible for perpetuating discord and undermining the unity of the believers, while the actual crime of the massacre of members of the Prophet's family receded into the "collective unconscious" as repressed memory of Muslims.

The collective guilt over such a monstrous crime as the massacre of the Prophet's family however cannot be washed away. In Freudian term the repression by Sunni Muslims of their collective memory turned into their collective neuroses. The pathology of violence among Muslims and Muslim violence directed at non-Muslims might be traced back to the record of violence—the war against apostasy, for instance, launched by Abu Bakr, the first Caliph, even as the Qur'an states categorically "There shall be no coercion in matters of faith" (2: 256)—and tribal conflicts culminating in Hussein's murder that stain the early years of Islamic history. In *Moses and Monotheism* Freud wrote,

> We must not forget that all the peoples who now excel in the practice of anti-Semitism became Christians only in relatively recent times, sometimes forced to it by bloody compulsion. One might say they all are "badly christened"; under the thin veneer of Christianity they have remained what their ancestors were, barbarically polytheistic. They have not yet overcome their grudge against the new religion which was forced on them, and they have projected it on to the source from which Christianity came to them. The facts that the Gospels tell a story which is enacted among Jews, and in truth treats only of Jews, has facilitated such a projection. The hatred for Judaism is at bottom hatred for Christianity, and it is not surprising that in the German National Socialist revolution this close connection of the two monotheistic religions finds such clear expression in the hostile treatment of both.[46]

Freud touched a raw nerve that is readily inflamed in speculating on the origins of genocidal European anti-Semitism. This hatred was imported into the Middle East, and Muslim

Judeophobia, or anti-Jew bigotry, present from pre-modern times "Islamized" it. But even though there was no basis or record of the sort of anti-Judaism in Islam or among Muslims that existed beneath the "thin veneer of Christianity" in Europe, yet the phenomenon of "badly christened" Christians has its parallel in the Islamic history of Bedouin Arabs outwardly accepting Islam without faith entering their hearts just as the Prophet was warned. The lesson from the Qur'anic reference to Bedouin Arabs lacking belief, as faith had not entered their hearts, apply to Muslims in general since their hypocrisy looms large despite repeated warnings about it in their sacred text. The customs of Bedouin Arabs remained unreformed despite, or because of, their forceful conversion and their repression in the war against apostasy launched by Abu Bakr following the Prophet's death. The Bedouin mentality left its pagan mark on the body politics of the Islamic civilization, since beneath the "thin veneer of Islam" the Bedouin culture remained resilient. Muslim Judeophobia in pre-modern times reflected tribal narrow-mindedness against the outsider, and the disdain shown towards Jews buttressed Arab and Muslim feelings of tribal or religious superiority contrary to the teachings of Islam. Moreover, given their collective neuroses and the repressed memory of violence anti-Jew bigotry provided Muslims with an excuse for blaming others for their own failings and a proclivity to look for a conspiracy by non-Muslims working against the idealized notion of Muslim unity, while denying the bleak reality of their own, self-generated tribal conflicts.

The world of Islam stretches far beyond the Arab region, or the Middle East with its diverse ethnicity of Afghans, Arabs, Berbers, Kurds, Iranians, Turks and more. The largest concentration of Muslim population is in South Asia, and the largest Muslim country is far away from the Middle East in Indonesia. Most Muslims outside of the Middle East have little or no personal contact with Jews, and only know of Jews through the lens of the religious-based history taught in the confines of their local religious schools and mosques. In modern times, Arab and Muslim anti-Semitism was exported from the Middle East to the wider world of Islam as religious propaganda sweetened by the largesse of petrodollars. Just as non-Arab and non-Middle Eastern Muslims defer to Arabs on Islam, so they have also readily absorbed without questioning the entire filth of anti-Semitism propagated by Arab hate-mongers. The result is the undeniable reality of the deplorable extent to which Islamist Judeophobia fused with genocidal European anti-Semitism has become part of contemporary Islam.

Islamism is a pathology propelling a significant segment of the global Muslim population into conflict with others—Jews being most prominent—viewed as enemies. Not paradoxically, this inner compulsion of Islamists to wage war against others has turned into Muslim-on-Muslim violence, a raging sectarian conflict of Sunnis against Shi'ites and ethnic conflicts of tribes against tribes or nations against nations. Islamists have shredded their "thin veneer of Islam" and displayed their "jihad" as a neo-pagan belief in the cult of violence. The world at the end of the twentieth century was not prepared to encounter Islamism as an ideology of hate and terror. The terrorist acts of war unleashed by Islamists on September 11, 2001 came as a shock. Since that fateful day the world has been informed about Islamists and the need to recall from history how violence born of Jew-hatred or anti-Semitism does not end with Jews, nor is it only about Jews. Anti-Semitism was, and remains, a plague that endangers all. There is an urgent need to quell, rather than appease, Muslim anti-Semitism. The suicidal acts of terrorism that Islamists have engaged in since the 2001 attacks on New York and Washington demonstrate their willingness, if they acquire the wherewithal, to bring about their own version of *Götterdämmerung* in their fanatical desire to destroy the enemy. The world since that September morning in 2001 has stood warned of the peril of Arab and Muslim anti-Semitism in the years ahead.

VI.

ISIS, Saudi Arabia and the West

> *In Islam violence is specifically the violence of the conqueror. Islam was imposed by force; it became a history of conquests.*
>
> Adonis[1]

In a hard-hitting essay on ISIS (Islamic State of Iraq and Syria) for London's the *Mail On Sunday* (22 March 2015), the 2001 Nobel Prize winning author, V.S. Naipaul, wrote, "ISIS could very credibly abandon the label of Caliphate and call itself the Fourth Reich." In watching ISIS unleash a bloody-minded rampage across the Fertile Crescent, Naipaul observed that the revival of "religious dogmas and deadly rivalries between Sunnis and Shi'as, Sunnis and Jews and Christians is a giant step into darkness." Naipaul's writings on Islam and Muslims in recent years, as in the books *Among the Believers* and *Beyond Belief*, have been quite the most incisive and penetrating in exploring the landscape of extremist politics of the global Islamist movement from inside the Muslim world.

Ever since the relatively obscure Abu Bakr al-Baghdadi stepped forth on the pulpit of the Great Mosque in Mosul, Iraq, on June 28, 2014 to announce the rebirth of the Caliphate (abolished in 1924 by the Turkish leader Mustafa Kemal Ataturk), with al-Baghdadi himself assuming the title as Caliph Ibrahim, the ruling head of the *ummah,* or worldwide community of Muslims, many would agree with Naipaul, despite the hyperbole, that "ISIS has to be seen as the most potent threat to the world since the Third Reich." Three years later and after a great deal of carnage wrought by ISIS, or *Daesh* (Dawlat al-Islamiyah f'al-Iraq wa Bilad al-Shams) in Arabic, the re-taking of Mosul by Iraqi forces in July 2017 after nearly nine months of fierce fighting that left the city mostly in ruin and the Grand Mosque destroyed, the more relevant question is not if ISIS has been smashed but what could be next. Though the self-declared Caliph Ibrahim, a.k.a. Abu Bakr al-Baghdadi, might be dead and buried in the ruins of Mosul, yet the sort of Islamism he represented—a creed of undiluted *jihād* related terror—continues to draw support within the world of Islam, while ISIS was the most recent iteration of Islamism.

We have seen the phenomenon of ISIS before this most recent episode of *jihādi* terror, and it was not as al-Qaeda's second coming. The first successful appearance of an ISIS in modern times was the whirlwind with which the Bedouin warriors of Abdulaziz ibn Saud (1876-1953) emerged from the interior of the Arabian Desert in 1902 to take hold of the main fortress in Riyadh, the local capital of the surrounding region known as Najd. Some twenty-four years later, this desert warrior-chief and his armies of Bedouin raiders defeated the ruling Sharifian house in the coastal province of Hejaz where Islam's two holy cities, Mecca and Medina, are located.

Husayn bin Ali (1854-1931), Sharif of Mecca and Emir of Hejaz, had joined his fate with the British against the Ottoman Empire during World War I. One of his sons, Prince Feisal, led the "Arab Revolt" for independence from Ottoman rule made famous by T.E. Lawrence (1888-1935). But in the aftermath of the Great War, which brought the Ottoman Empire to its ruin, Bedouin tribes in the interior of the Arabian Desert were jostling for power, and the House of Sharif Husayn proved inept at maintaining its own against threats posed to its rule over Hejaz, and as the *khadim* [steward] of the holy cities of Mecca and Medina.

Another Englishman, a counterpart to T.E. Lawrence ("Lawrence of Arabia"), was Harry St. John Philby (1885-1960), sent as a British agent during the Great War into the interior of the Arabian Desert. Philby would get to know Abdulaziz ibn Saud; eventually he worked for Ibn Saud as the warrior-chief rose in power and prominence. Philby chronicled the emergence of

Abdulaziz ibn Saud as "the greatest of all the kings of Arabia," and wrote the history of Ibn Saud's tribe and people under the title *Arabia of the Wahhabis*. In the West, ironically, Philby is better known as the father of Kim Philby, the Soviet double agent, instead of the confidant of the founder of modern Saudi Arabia. Philby apparently became Muslim, took the name of Abdullah, and lived among the Arabs.

The defeat of the Sharifian forces in Hejaz in 1925 cleared the path for Abdulaziz ibn Saud's eventual triumph in creating the eponymous Kingdom of Saudi Arabia. The fall of Mecca to the Bedouin warriors known as the *Ikhwān*, or the Brethren—(to be distinguished from the movement known as *Ikhwān al-Muslimīn* [Muslim Brotherhood] founded by the Egyptian Hasan al-Banna in 1928)—ended the ambition of Sharif Husayn and his sons to rule Arabia with the support of the British. The Sharifian defeat also meant that Britain would not have to referee the conflict between two of its allies—Sharif Husayn and his sons on one side, and Abdulaziz ibn Saud and his *Ikhwān* warriors on the other—competing for mastery over Arabia.

Philby's loyalty to Abdulaziz ibn Saud restrained him from mentioning the terror and havoc *Ikhwān* warriors perpetrated in the occupation of Hejaz and the capture of Mecca and Medina.[2] But he was effusive in describing what he viewed as the renewal of Islam's original revolution in the desert soil of its birth. He became the premier salesman of Abdulaziz ibn Saud and his family to the outside world, as T.E. Lawrence was of Prince Feisal and the Sharifian claims to rule the Arabs.[3] Philby wrote,

> Ibn Sa'ud made it clear from the beginning that he would tolerate no criticism of or interference with God's law on earth... On Friday, January 8th, 1926, in the Great Mosque of Mecca after the congregational prayers, Ibn Sa'ud was proclaimed King of the Hijaz with all the traditional ceremony prescribed by Islamic precedent. It was at once an act of faith and a challenge to the world: to be made good in due course, without deviation from

> the principle on which it was based, to the glory of God, of whose sustaining hand he was ever conscious amid all the vicissitudes of good and evil fortune, which in the long years to come were to lead his people, under his guidance, out of the wilderness into a promised land flowing with milk and honey. The great fight, of four and twenty years almost to the day, was over; and a greater span, by nearly four years, yet lay before him to develop the fruits of victory for the benefit of generations yet unborn: generations which 'knew not Joseph', nor ever heard the war-cry of the Ikhwan.[4]

ii.

The stated objective of the ISIS was apparently to remake the map of the Middle East drawn by Britain and France, as victorious powers in World War I, following the collapse of the Ottoman Empire in 1918. The goal was to unite the Fertile Crescent—the region between the eastern Mediterranean and the Persian Gulf—under the newly resurrected Caliphate's rule, where "God's law" rules without anyone's interference much as Saudi Arabia's founder, Abdulaziz ibn Saud, announced in 1926 on entering Mecca.

ISIS's self-proclaimed leader, Abu Bakr al-Baghdadi, in announcing the re-establishment of the Caliphate, set for ISIS a hugely ambitious program, even if it seemed anachronistic for Muslims in the twenty-first century. But ISIS's gamble to engineer the creation of the Caliphate and obliterate the post-WWI settlement was not entirely far-fetched when considered in the context of the making of Saudi Arabia. There was also the shared doctrine of the Wahhabi-Salafi interpretation of Islam, which Abdulaziz ibn Saud insisted, and so did ISIS insists, to be the only *true* Islam; all other versions and sects of Islam among Muslims were denounced as heresy or, worse, as apostasy, and violently punished.

The collapse of the Ottoman Empire let loose forces in the Middle East, some of which were contained by Britain and France in accordance with their Sykes-Picot Agreement of 1916. In the Arabian Peninsula, Britain kept in check the forces let loose, preventing their spill over into the Fertile Crescent, until one coalition of Bedouin warriors led by Abdulaziz ibn Saud emerged as clear winner over the territories previously held by Turkey in the Fertile Crescent.

The deep forbidding interior of the Arabian Peninsula consists of the highlands and desert of Najd, far removed from what were once the major centers of the Islamic civilization at its peak. Inhabited by Bedouin tribes, deeply conservative in their customs and manner of living, and disapproving of the ways of the outside world, Najd was a primitive backwater of the Middle East and was left on its own.

The emergence of Abdulaziz ibn Saud as the ruler of Najd and Hejaz in the 1920s, and then as the monarch of the Kingdom of Saudi Arabia under the watchful eyes of Britain as the hegemonic power in the Middle East after the World War I, was not merely the result of one coalition of Bedouin tribes trouncing its opponents for the spoils of war. It was also the victory of a doctrine—of Wahhabism,[5] to which Abdulaziz ibn Saud was wedded as a legacy of his family and tribal history, and which provided the religious and ideological legitimacy for the so-called "conservative revolution" or the Wahhabi version of Islamic "reform" he heralded in establishing his kingdom.

iii.

In the nine decades between the triumph of Abdulaziz ibn Saud and the rise of ISIS, Wahhabism emerged from the margins of the Muslim world to become the dominant face of Sunni Islam, which claims the allegiance of the vast majority of Muslims. This occurred as a result of Ibn Saud's instincts and the discovery of oil in his kingdom. As a warrior-chief, he knew his limits on how far to push against the interests of Britain; and when he negotiated the subsequent embrace of his kingdom and leadership by the United States, which replaced Britain as the protector of the regional order at the end of World War II.

History is filled with surprises, and so it is with the history of Wahhabism. Muslims who heard about it or encountered its practitioners during the nineteenth century, viewed it with disdain, yet it came to almost represent and somewhat define mainline Sunni Islam towards the end of the twentieth century. According to the historian Hamid Algar, "Wahhabism is essentially a movement without pedigree; it came out of nowhere in the sense not only of emerging from the wastelands of Najd, but also its lack of substantial precedent in Islamic history."[6]

The founder of Wahhabism, Muhammad ibn Abdul-Wahhab (1703-1791), was a Najdi born in a small town called `Ayaina. His grandfather had been the town's religious elder and *qādhi* (judge), and his father followed him. The founder was reputedly precocious in his religious education and, according to Philby's account, based upon what he learned in the service of Abdulaziz ibn Saud, "some of his forbears may well have known or heard the preaching of the famous Unitarian Ibn Taymiyyah, who was the main source of Muhammad ibn Abdul Wahhab's inspiration."[7]

By 1745, Abdul-Wahhab had acquired a reputation as teacher, preacher, and reformer, with religious training acquired by spending time in the holy city of Medina. Apparently committed to the moral and spiritual reform of fellow Muslims, he announced a program of commending virtue and condemning vice in his native city. While he acquired some followers, he also generated controversy and opposition among those who viewed his preaching as too literal and harsh. Eventually when asked to leave `Ayaina, he headed for Dar'iya in the neighbourhood of Riyadh, and there sealed a relationship with the local chief, Muhammad ibn Saud (?- 1765). Thus was born the historic alliance between the founder of what became the Wahhabi movement and the chief of the Saudi clan of central Arabia, whose progeny was Abdulaziz ibn Saud.

The main thrust of Abdul-Wahhab's "reformist" teaching was to purge his people's belief in Islam of what he considered superstitions. He denounced devotion to holy men as saints, forbade the care and respect for their tombs as places for visitations and prayers, and preached against reverence in general for the dead. Instead, he insisted on the literal and explicit meaning of the Qur'anic text, and of applying Qur'anic penalties, such as the cutting off the limbs of thieves and stoning of adulterers. He declared those who violated what he understood to be the teachings of the only *true* faith to be *mushrikīn* (idolaters), against whom *jihād* (holy war) was not merely permissible but obligatory: "their blood could legitimately be shed, their property was forfeit, and their women and children could be enslaved."[8] Abdul-Wahhab turned Ibn Taymiyya's doctrine of *takfīr* (of pronouncing anathema on his opponents) into a *jihādi* movement that would eventually culminate in the making of the Kingdom of Saudi Arabia.

At the time, Abdul-Wahhab's inclinations were reformist. According to one of the most respected Western scholars of Islam, Sir Hamilton Gibb, there remained those "pagan Arabs who accepted the dogmas of the Koran without completely giving up their old beliefs. What Muhammad [the prophet] did for them was to superimpose upon the deposit of Arabian animism a supreme controlling power in the personality and activity of an all-powerful God."[9] Abdul-Wahhab's "reformist" concern was apparently motivated by a loathing of the practices he railed against, as *shīrk* (idolatry), which he maintained contaminated the purity of Islam's strict monotheism.

Abdul-Wahhab's doctrinal solution was to "purify" Islam by insisting that any practice that detracts from—or interposes itself between—the unquestioning submission to God, was *shīrk* and, therefore, *haram* (forbidden). His uncompromising insistence on *tauhid* (Oneness or Unity of God) set the stark division between Islam and *kufr* (disbelief), and between Islam and *shīrk*. Abdul-Wahhab's precursor in this respect was Ibn Taymiyya (1263-1328), whose theology was shaped by the calamity of the Mongol invasion of the Arab world.

Ibn Taymiyya blamed the weakness and corruption of the Arab world on the borrowings from non-Muslims of un-Islamic ideas. These, he believed, had prepared the ground for the devastation brought upon Muslims by the Mongols. He saw the Mongol calamity as God's punishment visited upon Muslims for deviating from the true path of Islam. Ibn Taymiyya's enmity towards the Shi'ite Muslims as heretics, and his polemics against Christians as Trinitarians and, therefore, not strictly monotheists, laid the basis for the even narrower and more intolerant doctrine Abdul-Wahhab later preached in the arid and isolated environment of Najd.

Ibn Taymiyya's emphasis on *tauhid*, which inspired Abdul-Wahhab, was a warning for Muslims to beware of Christians and Shi'ite Muslims, whom he denounced as falsifying the true belief. Abdul-Wahhab extended Ibn Taymiyya's polemics and bigotry also against the Sufis devoted to the spiritual and mystical dimension of Islam, labeling them as deviationists or polytheists. In the end, Abdul-Wahhab's theology, mimicking that of Ibn Taymiyya, was characterized by the tendency to pronounce *takfīr* on Muslims: accusing them of apostasy or disbelief. As these accusations of apostasy spread, they provoked among Muslims irreparable disagreements, which the followers of Abdul-Wahhab would seize upon as *casus belli* for their *jihād*.

The "reform" of Abdul-Wahhab to "purify" Islam was a return to the imagined simplicity of the early years, when Muhammad preached against idol worship among the Arabs. Abdul-Wahhab spurned the traditional consensus of the *ulema* (religious scholars) and the *fuqāha* (jurists) that had been worked out between the seventh and the thirteenth centuries, referred to as the classical period of Islam.[10] This consensus reflected the highest achievement of Muslims. Through cultural exchanges, Islam was emerging from its native and backward environment of Arabia, far removed from ancient civilizations of the Eastern Roman Empire (Byzantine) and Persia. Despite wars, the Islamic civilization was shaped over the remains of empires that Arab armies had defeated. Gibb explained,

> After the end of the Arab-Muslim conquests there was a period of three centuries during which the territorial spread of Islam, though vast indeed, remained practically stable. This gave time and opportunity for a thorough interpenetration of the religious attitudes and beliefs of the original Arab immigrants and of the peoples with whom they mixed to form the medieval Muslim nation. In the course of these centuries, after a long stage of theological disputes, a certain equilibrium was reached. The theology of Islam was established in logical and rational terms, and this achievement did something to counteract the influence of grosser superstitions.[11]

After the death of Muhammad in 632, Arabs and Muslims had swept forth into the world. The Prophet had accomplished his mission of implanting among the pagan Arabs the worship of One God, in Arabic *Allah*, the God of Abraham as the Qur'an repeatedly affirms. Upon his death, the future of Islam and Muslims was an open book with blank pages to be filled in. But there was no heavenly mandate for the role of Caliph (*khalif* in Arabic, meaning successor), or for wars of conquests or empire. These came about as innovation, and as military offensives defeated far superior and more cultured adversaries. Justifications for such innovations (for instance, the office of Caliph) and military conquests were found in retrospect, or discovered, or invented—based on the Quran or on the oral reports of the life and practice of the Prophet (*hadīth*), which Muslims came to accept as normative. Within a generation of the Prophet's demise, his successors, under the title of Caliph, became rulers of empire. Their pomp and power rivalled, and often exceeded, those of the Byzantine and Persian rulers.

Islam, as faith and submission to the idea of One God, evolved into Islam as civilization, and there arose the necessity of reconciling the two. Devising the administration of empire became the task of the early generation of learned Muslims. In the context of the ancient world, their achievements were significant. The high standing the Islamic civilization achieved during the classical period of Arab and Muslim history later acquired a near-sacred status in the imagination of generations of Muslims up to the present times.

As centers of the high Islamic civilization, except for the revered status of the two holy cities of Mecca and Medina, became located outside of Arabia, the rest of Arabia once more became the backwater of civilization. From the remoteness of Najd, the contents of the high Islamic civilization could be thought of as departures from the prophetic era, and as corrupting Islam.

Abdul-Wahhab came to consider developments that distanced Muslims from the simplicity of early Islam as innovations, and since innovations (*al-bid'āh*), in his austere view, brought corruption, he denounced any innovation unacceptable as deviation or heresy. Abdul-Wahhab's doctrine was thus repudiation of traditional Islam as represented by the highest authority in the Caliphate, and of the shared consensus of the mainline Muslim scholars of his time. His alliance, cemented in 1745, with Muhammad ibn Saud, started the *jihād* he evidently wanted to wage against those Muslims he denounced as deviants for refusing to accept his doctrine. For the next half-century, the Saudi-Wahhabi alliance nearly succeeded in the conquest of most of Arabia.

Muhammad ibn Saud died in 1765. Abdul-Aziz succeeded his father and with the approval and blessings of Abdul-Wahhab, who died in 1791, he waged zealously the *jihād* his father had begun. In 1803 Abdul-Aziz's warriors, under the command of his son

Sa'ud, took Hejaz and entered Mecca. There they repeated what they had done earlier in Iraq. In Philby's account,

> [Sa'ud] suddenly appeared before the holy town of Karbala [the site where Husain, the grandson of the prophet and venerated by the Shi'ites as their third Imam, was brutally killed by the Arab army of the Caliph in Damascus in 680 A.D.] in March 1802. After a short siege it was carried by storm, and given over to slaughter and pillage; the inhabitants were killed without mercy in the streets and houses; the great dome of the tomb of Husain was demolished, and the bejeweled covering of his grave carried off as spoil; and everything of value in the town was collected and taken off to the watering of al Abyadh, near Samawa, where Sa'ud settled down for a space to count his gains and distribute them in the traditional manner. He then returned to Dar'iya to receive the congratulations of his father and his people on the first doughty blow struck in the service of the true faith against a dispensation which was regarded in Wahhabi eyes as the incarnation of infidelity. It was certainly an act that shocked the world far beyond the limits of the Shia' persuasion: and may be regarded as the starting-point of a general revulsion against Wahhabism, which was to have disastrous consequences for the Wahhabi State. But there was only joy in Dar'iya without reserve; and the pattern set at Karbala was soon to be copied in the holy cities of the Hijaz before the tide of retribution began to flow.[12]

Revulsion against Wahhabism, as Philby wrote, eventually moved the Ottoman Empire to act. The sack of Mecca by the Wahhabis was a mighty slap on the face of the Caliph in Istanbul and, despite the strains on the resources of the Ottoman rulers since the French invasion of Egypt under Napoleon's command in 1798, an Ottoman army was raised and sent by Egypt's governor, Muhammad Ali Pasha, into Arabia.

The Saudi-Wahhabi warriors were driven out of Hejaz by the soldiers of the Caliph, the ruler of the Ottoman Empire, and Mecca was re-captured in the early months of 1813, bringing an end to Wahhabi rule in the two holiest cities of Islam. The Ottoman army then pushed forward by stages into the interior of Arabia. The

Saudi-Wahhabi stronghold of Dar'iya capitulated in September 1818. The power of the Saudi-Wahhabi alliance was broken; Hejaz was restored to the rule of the Ottoman Caliphate; and Mecca returned to the stewardship of the House to which Husayn bin Ali [Sharif Husayn] belonged.[13]

The defeat of Saudi-Wahhabi power confined Wahhabism to the interior of the Najdi desert. The restoration of Ottoman rule in Hejaz also meant restoring in Mecca the traditional Islamic consensus reached by the *ulema* during the classical period of Muslim history. Wahhabism—an aberration of primitive minds far removed from, and suspicious of, civilization—was destined to pass into history as a footnote, but for the fatal error of the Ottoman rulers in entering the Great War in 1914 on the side of Germany and the Austro-Hungarian Empire.

iv.

The conquest of Arabia by Abdulaziz ibn Saud and his *Ikhwan* warriors in the first quarter of the twentieth century was cruel and bloody. It also occurred under the gaze of the British in the region, and the material support Britain provided at critical stages of the march of the Saudi-Wahhabi warrior-chief, Abdulaziz ibn Saud, to power.

The English created a myth that Abdulaziz ibn Saud was a great unifier of the tribes of Arabia. Philby was at the head of those who spun their tales of the Saudi warrior as among the greatest of the Arab leaders, even going to the absurd length of comparing him to the Prophet of Islam. "Like the Prophet Muhammad," Philby wrote, "Abdul-`Aziz ibn Sa'ud was also a man of destiny."[14]

The facts were alarmingly opposite. Abdulaziz ibn Saud massacred his way to conquering Arabia. In towns such as Taif, Bureida and Al Huda, the Wahhabi *Ikhwān* slaughtered the townspeople. They tried to destroy the tomb of the Prophet in Medina and desecrated cemeteries in Mecca. They also spread death and devastation among Shi'ite Muslims in the eastern parts of the Arabian Peninsula. Hatred for Shi'ism as heresy is deeply rooted in the Wahhabi doctrine. Wahhabis believe that Shi'a reverence for Ali, cousin and son-in-law of the Prophet, as Imam (religious leader) has made Ali co-equal to the Prophet or placed Ali even ahead of the Prophet, thereby committing the unforgivable transgression of *shīrk*, or polytheism.

The *Ikhwān* of Abdulaziz ibn Saud were checked from raiding towns in Iraq—and pillaging Shi'ite holy cities of Karbala and Najaf, as the Wahhabi warriors had done in the early nineteenth century—by the frontier marked out between Arabia and Iraq by Sir Percy Cox, the British High Commissioner in the Persian Gulf region after World War I. Despite the efforts of Saudi apologists, both native and Western, to airbrush and erase the horrors perpetrated by Abdulaziz ibn Saud and his army in subduing the tribes of Arabia, the memory of that gory history persists. Saïd K. Aburish, an Arab historian and journalist, remarked:

> It was an atmosphere where the sword of the executioner had a recognizable name, the *rakban*, or "necker," and it was well known and feared as the guillotine during the French Revolution... No fewer than 400,000 people were killed and wounded, for the Ikhwan did not take prisoners, but mostly killed the vanquished. Well over a million inhabitants of the territories conquered by Ibn Saud fled to other countries: Iraq, Syria, Egypt, Jordan and Kuwait.[15]

Fortune, however, smiled on Abdulaziz ibn Saud, as the discovery of plentiful oil transformed the status of his kingdom in the strategic thinking of Western powers and the newly formed states in the region. But first he had to settle the tensions within his coalition of the *Ikhwān* warriors, grown suspicious that he might be turning his back on them. The intolerance of others is a defining characteristic of the Wahhabi doctrine and its adherents. They saw his increasingly close relationship with the British, even willingness to be instructed by them as their paid agent, disapprovingly.

Abdulaziz ibn Saud sought to pacify the leaders of the *Ikhwān* in his entourage with gold and other forms of wealth. He told them to go back to their women and their homes, and enjoy the largesse he readily offered them. He advised them that with the conquest of Arabia attained, there could be no further role for *ghazzu* (the customary Bedouin practice of raiding), as in the past. Yet, as he failed to win over the hardliners among the *Ikhwān*, a showdown became unavoidable. In March 1929, Abdulaziz Ibn Saud and his loyal warriors confronted the dissident *Ikhwān* veterans outside the village of Sabila, and offered them one final gesture of reconciliation by asking them to surrender peacefully and return to their homes. The offer was refused, and the king ordered his men to mow down the opposition with their British-supplied machine guns. Some five thousand *Ikhwān* mutineers were killed; the rest fled to Iraq and Kuwait, only to be pushed out in the open by the authorities and bombed by Britain's Royal Air Force.[16]

This explosive tension at the heart of the Saudi-Wahhabi partnership remains; it is essentially irresolvable. Although it may be managed or contained, there is no moderation, nor any allowed. The Wahhabi doctrine is fundamentally intolerant of others, especially of Muslims who reject Wahhabism. This doctrinally-based bigotry leaves Wahhabis at unease with anyone who does not share their creed, and fearful of alien cultures contaminating or undermining their own closed tribal ways. According to Hamid Algar, there is "a fear of perceived deviation at the very heart of Wahhabism and helps to explain its intrinsically censorious nature."[17]

Abdulaziz ibn Saud dealt with the *Ikhwān* mutineers in the customary manner of the tribal code of retribution: he executed them. Those among the *Ikhwān* warriors who remained loyal, he recruited into what eventually became the National Guards, the trusted militia of the Saudi-Wahhabi partnership. However, the ghosts of the *Ikhwān* mutineers mowed down in Sabila have haunted the kingdom. Their grievance against the ruling House of Saud is occasionally aroused by what is sometimes regarded as its too intimate embrace of Western powers.

In the second half of the twentieth century, oil made Saudi Arabia and its rulers unimaginably wealthy. It was also a double-edged sword: threats to the Saudi kingdom mounted. The earnings from oil were "rental" income, received from sale of a natural resource that required very little native ingenuity or work. As the earnings mushroomed, the headache for the Saudi rulers came from the dilemma of how to administer this massive infusion of petrodollars without disrupting too flagrantly the Wahhabi-approved customs of the kingdom. This felicitous headache was compounded by the envy of non-Saudi Arabs; by the appeal of secular nationalism across the Arab Middle East; and by migrant foreign workers needed in large numbers to meet the labor shortage triggered by the construction boom. Native Saudis, who received a subsidy, lacked incentive to work. Consequently, the kingdom had to cope with the presence of foreign workers who wanted equitable treatment based on international standards, in a country wary of all things foreign.

Change is both unavoidable and disruptive, irrespective of how it is managed or checked. In awakening to the modern world with its pressures for change, Saudi Arabia was set on a collision course between the old and the new. Since emerging as a central player in the global economy, given its immense oil reserves and potential new discoveries, the kingdom nevertheless has remained mysterious to outsiders. As John R. Bradley, a Western journalist who lived and worked there, observed, "The Kingdom of Saudi Arabia, so extraordinarily introverted and completely closed to outsiders, is perhaps the world's last great, forbidden country."[18]

Hence, those whom Saudi largesse would not appease grew loud in their denunciations of the corrupting influence of the new ways. The ghosts of the *Ikhwān* mutineers worked their spell, and Juhayman al-Utaybi, a hardline Wahhabi who had served in the National Guard, gathered others around him to strike at the heart of Islam's sacred institution, the Grand Mosque of Mecca, which the Saudi dynasty is sworn to protect. Al-Utaybi came to believe that since the House of Saud was corrupt, it had lost its legitimacy to rule Arabia. His father and grandfather were *Ikhwān* warriors who had participated in the rebellion against Abdulaziz ibn Saud on the battlefield of Sabila. He recalled the grievance of the *Ikhwān* against their king for turning soft on Wahhabi principles; by the time he plotted his own rebellion, the signs of Saudi deviation appeared to many devoted Wahhabis as too pronounced.

The evening of November 20, 1979 marked the beginning of the year 1400 in the Islamic calendar. On that night, al-Utaybi led his supporters to incite a general Wahhabi-led uprising against the Saudi rulers by seizing the Grand Mosque in Mecca, where Muslim pilgrims from around the world gather for their annual pilgrimage, the Hajj. The rebellion was crushed and al-Utaybi was executed, along with those of his followers captured with him in the Grand Mosque. But the rebellion, although it was likely doomed to fail, revealed that the most lethal threat to the kingdom remains internal. It arises from the contradiction at the heart of the Saudi-Wahhabi partnership: the Wahhabi fear of deviation as the Saudi rulers seek to administer the kingdom awash with petrodollars and pressed by the forces of change on all sides.

V.

Al-Utaybi's rebellion against the House of Saud was hushed up by the Saudi-Wahhabi authorities, and pushed down the memory hole of Muslims and non-Muslims alike. According to Yaroslav

Trofimov, author of *The Siege of Mecca*, "In the years after the Mecca uprising, the Saudi government tried its best to erase these bloody events from public memory. The subject of Juhayman remains taboo in the kingdom, strenuously avoided by Saudi historians and ignored by official textbooks."[19]

There were, however, other events in the Middle East and beyond in 1979 of even greater immediate consequences than the siege in Mecca. In February of that year, the Shah of Iran left Tehran in the wake of a revolution that turned Islamic, and which brought an old Shi'ite cleric, Ayatollah Ruhollah Khomeini (1902-89), back from exile in Najaf, Iraq, and via Paris, France, to become its leader. Then, on November 4, two weeks before the siege of Mecca occurred, hardline student followers of Khomeini stormed the U.S. embassy in Tehran and took American diplomats as hostages. The Americans would be held for 444 days, before their release in January 1981.

Additionally, in December 1979 came the invasion of Afghanistan by the Soviet Union. It sparked a near decade-long Soviet-Afghan war, which also became—at the beginning of Islam's fifteenth century—a holy war or *jihād* of Muslims supported by the United States against infidels. It set the stage for the eventual disintegration of the Soviet Union in December 1991, bringing to an end the Cold War, which for nearly half a century had defined the main security tension between the East (communism) and the West (capitalism) in global politics. The Afghan war also became the cradle for the next generation of *jihādi* warriors and terrorists that would erupt on the global stage after the attacks of September 11, 2001 on the World Trade Center in New York City and the Pentagon in Washington.

The making of the Islamic Republic of Iran in the Middle East upset the regional equilibrium between monarchies and republican states. The ruling Shi'ite clerics in Tehran broadcast their intent to export the Islamic revolution; they provocatively gestured to Shi'ite Muslims in neighboring Arab states to create a common front with Palestinians and other disenfranchised segments of the population against Israel and undemocratic regimes headed by Sunni dictators and dynastic rulers in the Gulf region.

Saddam Hussein, the Sunni despot in Baghdad, felt the tremors of the Iranian revolution most intensely. His "republic of fear," as the Iraqi Shi'ite author and dissident, Kanan Makiya, described Saddam's Iraq, was a narrowly based autocratic regime drawing upon the sectarian loyalties of Sunni tribes in a state where Shi'ite Muslims made up two-thirds of the population.

Iran's revolutionary threat, although also feared by Sunni rulers of the Gulf states, including the House of Saud, was left to the Iraqi leader to countermand. Saddam Hussein viewed himself as leader and defender of the "Arab nation," and as the successor to the place that Egypt's Gamal Abdel Nasser once held in the imagination of Arabs. In his view, and in the opinion of most Arabs, Egypt's President Anwar Sadat had betrayed Nasser and the "Arab nation" by going to Jerusalem in November 1977 and making peace with Israel.

Saddam Hussein launched a pre-emptive war against Iran in September 1980. He hoped that by striking at Iran, still unsettled after the upheavals of the revolution, a regime change in Tehran might be brought about. It was a huge miscalculation. After the initial shock, Iran went on the offensive. The Iran-Iraq war turned into a nearly eight year grinding waste of men and materiel, finally ending in August 1988 with a UN-brokered ceasefire.

vi.

History is filled with unintended consequences. In retrospect, the Soviet-Afghan war and the Iran-Iraq war of the 1980s prepared the conditions for the explosive events of September 11, 2001 and after.

The Iran-Iraq War left the Iraqi despot, Saddam Hussein, in a terrible dilemma. His recklessness exposed him as vainglorious and foolish. It also left him in severe debt to those Arabs, in particular the Saudis and the Kuwaitis, who had bankrolled with their petrodollars his war against Iran. When Saddam Hussein requested debt forgiveness, the ruling house of Kuwait declined.

Saddam Hussein could not stomach the response of the Emir of Kuwait—it rankled him as ingratitude. He had taken Iraq to war against Khomeini's Iran in defense of Arabs and Sunni Islam against the Persians and their Shi'ite heresy. The Kuwaiti Emir's ingratitude could not go unpunished; consequently, Saddam Hussein dispatched his army to take over Kuwait. The raging folly of Saddam Hussein set the stage for the U.S.-led first Gulf War of February 1991—Operation Desert Storm—to liberate Kuwait and defend Saudi Arabia.

vii.

Abdulaziz ibn Saud, whose career had spanned the first five decades of the twentieth century, died in 1953. His legacy was to leave the second Saudi-Wahhabi state, named the Kingdom of Saudi Arabia—the first Saudi-Wahhabi state was launched by Muhammad ibn Saud and Abdul-Wahhab, in the mid-18th century—in the care of the House of Saud he had restored, by ruthlessness and cunning, to power. Since his death, his sons Saud, Feisal, Khalid, Fahd, Abdullah, and Salman have successively ruled the Kingdom.

The Kingdom of Saudi Arabia, when founded, was hugely anachronistic, a throwback to the values and customs of the seventh century in an age defined by science and man's quest for knowledge and adventure beyond his planetary home. The Kingdom of Saudi Arabia remains a bundle of contradictions held together from within by a religious doctrine—Wahhabism—

violently imposed and defended from the outside by the protective shield the United States has provided.

The famous photograph of Abdulaziz ibn Saud meeting with President Franklin Roosevelt in February 1945 aboard the U.S.S. *Quincy* symbolizes the incongruity of the Saudi-American "special relationship." About the meaning of this relationship to the Saudi rulers, Prince Feisal, Abdulaziz ibn Saud's son, remarked to President John Kennedy in 1962, "After Allah, we trust the United States."[20]

In the absence of oil, it is unlikely there would have been any relationship of the sort that the United States cultivated with the House of Saud. Saudi Arabia is a totalitarian state under the banner of Allah, and protected, as if Allah arranged it, by the United States. This special relationship, however, rests uneasily upon the minds of those Saudis who take their Wahhabism seriously and are offended by any real or perceived dilution of, or deviation from, their creed.

Fahd (1922-2005), the fourth son of Abdulaziz ibn Saud, succeeded his brother Khalid as king in 1982. With Saddam Hussein's army driving into Kuwait in August 1990, the threat to Saudi Arabia seemed imminent. Fahd approved the deployment of American forces inside the kingdom with the consent of the blind Sheik, Abdul Aziz Bin Baz, the Chief Mufti and the highest juridical authority in the kingdom, and other leading Wahhabi clerics.

Approval for stationing American forces inside Saudi Arabia carried a certain amount of risk, despite the support of the Wahhabi religious leaders. In one of his many private conversations with Philby, Abdulaziz ibn Saud had confided his views about Christianity and Christians; his remarks revealed the strange thinking of his people. On the basis of Philby's private papers, his biographer, Elizabeth Monroe, repeated those conversations between Abdulaziz ibn Saud and his English confidant, Philby:

> He [Abdulaziz ibn Saud] told Philby that by his standards Christians were of a kindred faith because they were 'people of the Book'; being believers according to their lights, they were less abhorrent to him than lax Muslims—*mushriqin*, or people who associate other beings such as saints with the worship of God. Purity of faith was more important to him than all else; the easy-going habits of the Hijazis and the Turks, with their acceptance of corruptions unknown to early Islam, their deviations into heretical byways, their veneration of shrines and their tolerance of music, smoking, and strong drink were anathema to him and to his people... By no means all believers agreed with him about Christians or about the possible wisdom of helping the British. To some of his men, all Christians were dogs, unfit to eat with or even to speak to, and he, by dealing with them, was as reprehensible as the Sharif... But he was not lax; he was a reformer and by extending his territory he was spreading the faith as first conceived. Christian allies were permissible if alliance served Islamic ends.[21]

What mattered to Abdulaziz ibn Saud, and to the House of Saud since the founder's rule, in accepting Christian support was if such support served Wahhabism. This same thinking could also apply to an alliance with Jews and Israel in defending Saudi interests, should such need arise.

There were, however, those Saudis who viewed the American military as a Christian-Jewish Crusader army, violating the purity and sacredness of the land with the two holiest cities of Islam. To hardline Wahhabis, the sight of American soldiers on Saudi soil was intolerable. The unintended consequence of the American-led liberation of Kuwait and defense of Saudi Arabia was the hardening of denunciation of the House of Saud by discontented Saudi Wahhabis.

In May 1991, a body of oppositionist Wahhabi theologians sent a letter to Sheikh Bin Baz. The main thrust of the letter was that the dependence of the kingdom for its security on foreign non-Muslim armies was evidence that the House of Saud had renounced *true* Islam. The letter was alarming. The criticism had come from within the Saudi society, and it revealed a widening gap between those Wahhabi theologians defending the Saudi-Wahhabi alliance, and those increasingly critical of the House of Saud for laxity.

Among the Wahhabi critics of Saudi rulers, Bin Baz heard from Osama bin Laden. In an open letter published in mid-1990s, Bin Laden rebuked the Wahhabi religious leaders for approving the decision of King Fahd to invite American forces into Saudi Arabia. He denounced this as a recipe for disaster for the Muslim *ummah* or community, and condemned the Saudi-Wahhabi alliance as that of apostates collaborating with Western powers.[22]

By the time Osama bin Laden wrote to Sheik Bin Baz, a profound change in the radical discourse of religion and politics within the Muslim world had occurred. Two apparently separate currents of extremist Muslim or Islamist thinking had merged; ironically, the House of Saud had been instrumental in bringing them about.

One current was the Wahhabi doctrine, from its inception onwards doctrinally located at the margins of Sunni Islam. The vast majority of Sunni Muslims viewed Wahhabism with disdain, as an extremist, life-denying perversion of traditional Islam, and as inherently bigoted and violent. But as Saudi money poured forth, spreading Wahhabi theology across the Muslim world and into the West, the House of Saud, flush with petrodollars, gradually altered the mainstream Sunni Muslim view of Wahhabism as perversion of Islam.

The other current was the innovation in Muslim thought presented by the Egyptian, Hasan al-Banna (1906-49), as the founder of the *Ikhwān al-Muslimīn* (the Muslim Brotherhood). The other Egyptian responsible for the brand of extremist theology associated with the Muslim Brotherhood was Sayyid Qutb (1906-66); his influence as the ideologue of radical Islam, or Islamism, among a new generation of Muslims born in the aftermath of the 1967 Arab-Israeli war, exceeded that of al-Banna.[23] While Hasan al-Banna and Sayyid Qutb were contemporaries and were both influenced by political developments in Europe between the two world wars, Qutb, unlike al-Banna, also experienced military rule in Egypt under Gamal Abdel Nasser and drew upon this experience—he was eventually imprisoned and executed by hanging in August 1966 by Nasser's regime—to deepen the Islamist critique of secular regimes in the Muslim world.

The defeat of the Ottoman Empire in the Great War, followed by the abolition of the Caliphate, had left pious Muslims at a loss. For the next half-century, politics in the Muslim world was primarily driven by secular nationalism and the pressures to modernize traditional societies in imitation of the West. But there were also persistent questions raging below the surface, in opposition to those in power, on how to return—"reform"—Muslim societies back to their authentic Islamic roots.

The Islamist answer was that corrupting influences had taken hold of the Muslim *ummah* long before the Western powers conquered Muslim lands. The writings of Ibn Taymiyya were revived, and his theology updated as an explanation of why the Muslim *ummah* in modern times was broken and distraught. Hasan al-Banna saw himself and the movement he founded as deepening and broadening the "reformist" ideas inherited from an earlier generation of thinkers and activists, such as Muhammad `Abduh (1849-1905) and Muhammad Rashid Rida (1865-1935).

Rashid Rida was an advocate of Islamic reform by which he meant a return to the Prophetic traditions of the earliest period, or of the first three generations of Muslims—*al-salāf al-salih* (pious ancestors). From this advocacy emerged the idea of "Salafism," which in turn became the hallmark of the Muslim Brotherhood and its offshoots across the Muslim world.[24] Salafism and Wahhabism were doctrinally convergent; members of the Muslim Brotherhood, once the Saudi kingdom was established, found their staunchest ally and financiers in the House of Saud and among the Wahhabi clerics. As the Canadian scholar of Islam and Muslim history, Professor Wilfred Cantwell Smith, noted, the *Salafiyah* movement, led, in "willingly accepting Wahhabi influence, to a reinvigorated fundamentalist activism" in the twentieth century.[25]

Hasan al-Banna and Sayyid Qutb, in turn, deepened the Wahhabi doctrine pertaining to the notion of *jihād*, and broadened its appeal for Muslims by preaching *jihād* as an obligatory duty for them. This duty was not, as Sayyid Qutb described in *Milestones* (the most widely read ideological text of Islamism), merely a matter of personal striving for self-improvement; it was, instead, engagement in the holy war to establish God's law on earth. In Sayyid Qutb's description, "Islam is the way of life ordained by God for all mankind... and orders practical life in all its daily details. Jihaad in Islam is simply a name for striving to make this system of life dominant in the world."[26] For Qutb, *jihād* as holy war was not simply one of the central pillars of Islam; it was inseparable from the meaning and practice of Islam.

For Hasan al-Banna, the allure of death and dying for Islam was ennobling. He wrote about the "art of death" (*fann al-mawt*), and how "God grants a 'noble life' to that nation alone which 'knows how to die a noble death.'"[27] In Hasan al-Banna's preaching of *jihād*, to be *truly* Muslim required seeking martyrdom. With such sermonizing, which made martyrdom for Muslims a desired goal, the path was paved for homicidal acts carried out by individuals willing to die in *jihād* for spreading Islam.

In the age of totalitarianism—which flourished in the twentieth century under the various headings of Marxism-Leninism, Stalinism, Hitler's National Socialism and Maoism—Hasan al-Banna and Sayyid Qutb added Islamism. Shariah, as God's law, in covering and monitoring every detail of human conduct, as Qutb insisted, is total; its enforcement through *jihād* made for an ideology—Islamism—consistent with the temperament of the totalitarian era. Islamism in its Shi'ite version, as

Khomeinism, triumphed in Iran with the establishment of the Islamic Republic.

Among Sunni Muslims, Islamism spurred the jihadist activities of the Muslim Brotherhood and its offshoots within Egypt, among Palestinians, and in North Africa among Algerians. Armed *jihād* became a freelancing activity of Muslims wherever many, or even a few, gathered and raised the banner of fighting for the honor, or for the spread, of Islam.

In October 1981, a cell of *jihādi* soldiers within the Egyptian army killed President Anwar Sadat for his "betrayal of Islam" in embracing Israeli leaders, and for signing a peace treaty with the Jewish state. It was in Afghanistan, however, during the Soviet-Afghan war of the 1980s, that *jihād* as a theology and totalitarian ideology, in other words as Islamism, came to its own. That *jihād* was the result of a collaborative effort of Salafist-Wahhabi warriors and volunteer recruits, financed by the House of Saud, Saudi citizens, and Gulf petrodollars, and armed with weapons from friendly states, including the United States.

viii.

The Soviet-Afghan war, or the Afghan *jihād* as it came to be known, hugely emboldened the Islamist movement. In Osama bin Laden it found its figurehead, its chief organizer, and its principal financier. In March 1997, Bin Laden gave an interview to Peter Arnett of the CNN in Jalalabad, Afghanistan. In response to Arnett's question about the significance of the Afghan *jihād*, Bin Laden answered:

> The influence of the Afghan *jihad* on the Islamic world was so great; it necessitated that people should rise above many of their differences and unite their efforts against their enemy... As for the young men who participated in *jihad* here, their number was quite big, praise and gratitude be to Him, and they spread in every place in which non-believers' injustice is perpetuated against Muslims. Their going to Bosnia, Chechnya, Tajikistan

> and other countries is but a fulfillment of a duty, because we believe that these states are part of the Islamic world.[28]

Bin Laden organized al Qaeda as the base for supporting the network of Islamist warriors in the global *jihād* he planned to ignite.

The unfolding confusion in world politics after the disintegration of the Soviet Union, the end of the Cold War, the beginning of the crack-up in the Middle East that followed the Gulf War of 1991, and the effects of the Balkan wars on Muslim opinion converged and assisted Bin Laden's plan to keep increasing *jihādi* pressure on the American presence inside Saudi Arabia and within the Middle East by striking at American installations and personnel. By the time Bin Laden gave his CNN interview, he had figured out the dynamics of a "virtuous circle" in the tactics and strategy of the global *jihād*. According to Jason Burke,

> Successful attacks would bring in recruits, money and prestige and mobilize and radicalize the 'Arab street.' [Bin Laden's] enhanced capability would then allow more successful attacks, which would accelerate the process. His aim had always been to instigate. When the situation had become sufficiently radicalized, his own interventions would be unnecessary. The Muslim youth would have cast off their illusions, embraced the true Islamic path and launched their own attacks against the tyrannical oppressors.[29]

In giving the 1997 CNN interview, Bin Laden and his inner circle of al Qaeda militants also understood the importance of the media in the dynamics of the "virtuous circle." As news organizations broadcast terrorist attacks claimed by al Qaeda, it would generate new recruits and funds for the *jihādi* terrorist network; and the greater or more outrageous the terrorist attacks on civilian and military targets, more time the media would spend on reporting them, further raising the profile of Bin Laden and al Qaeda among Muslims worldwide.

The September 11, 2001 attacks on the twin towers of the World Trade Center in New York, and the Pentagon in Washington, were spectacular in planning and execution; and the visual effects stunning to the global audience, as the world media broadcast the towers brought down in flames after al Qaeda *jihādi* terrorists had flown hijacked airplanes into them. A few weeks after September 11, Bin Laden spoke with Taysir Alluni, reporting from Kabul, Afghanistan, for the Qatar based television news *Al-Jazeera*. Bin Laden volunteered, "I say that the events that happened on Tuesday September 11 in New York and Washington are truly great events by any measure, and their repercussions are not yet over."[30] Osama bin Laden had exceeded even his own expectations to provoke the United States as the "Great Satan"—the appellation used by Iran's Khomeini—in going to war in the Muslim world.

Bin Laden instigated two wars: the second Afghan war and the war in Iraq for regime change. He had drawn American troops into the vortex of the Middle East as the catalyst for radical change at the center of Arab Islam, and to raise the stakes for the House of Saud as apostate collaborator with the "Great Satan." He likely suspected that the hunt for him might lead to his being killed, as it eventually did, when the U.S. Navy SEALs killed him in his hideout in Abbottabad, Pakistan, on May 2, 2011. But to his followers, Osama bin Laden had blazed the path of martyrdom.

In December 2004, Bin Laden had posted, on the website of the Global Islamic Media Front, the most damning indictment of the House of Saud. There was no longer any ambiguity in the message he was sending to his *jihādi* followers, and no effort was made to soften his critique of the rulers of Saudi Arabia. He declared,

> The Saudi regime has committed very serious acts of disobedience—worse than the sins and offenses that are contrary to Islam, worse than oppressing slaves, depriving them of their rights and insulting their dignity, intelligence, and feelings, worse than squandering the general wealth of the

> nation... It has got to the point where the regime has gone so far as to be clearly beyond the pale of Islam, allying itself with infidel America and aiding it against Muslims, and making itself an equal to God by legislating on what is or is not permissible without consulting God.[31]

Since 1945, at the end of the Second World War, conflicts of varying sorts and intensities had raged across the Middle East. The establishment of Israel in 1948 was followed by a series of Arab-Israeli wars, and the Arab/Palestinian-Israeli conflict has persisted despite the efforts of the great powers to find an acceptable settlement for both Jews and Palestinians. The Arab-Israeli wars, however, have paled in intensity and casualty figures beside the conflicts within the Arab world and the Iran-Iraq war of the 1980s. Through the decades, during these intra- and inter-Arab conflicts, Saudi Arabia remained more or less protected with American support.

The rebellion led by al-Utaybi in November 1979, however, revealed the internal fissures in Saudi society, which when ignited could lead to a bigger conflagration. Osama bin Laden understood this internal reality of the country of his birth. In striking at the distant enemy—the United States—on September 11, 2001, he lit the fuse inside Saudi Arabia. One of the most insightful scholars of Arab politics, Professor Fouad Ajami (1945-2014), an Arab-American, in 2004 remarked:

> It was a matter of time before the terrible wind that originated in the Arabian Peninsula returned to its point of origin. The jihadists had struck far and wide. They had taken the Wahhabi creed, stretched it to the breaking point, and turned it into an instrument of combat. Where the creed had once taught obedience to the rulers, it now turned its wrath on the 'infidels' defiling the sacred earth of Arabia. In Arabia, it was a time of denial. In the year behind us, the bubble in which the Saudi kingdom was sheltered burst, and today there is a running war between the forces of order and zealots who have put down roots in a realm that once thought car bombs and kidnapping were the lots of other lands.[32]

Few in the West, and even fewer in the United States, had any inkling of Ajami's reference in describing what Osama bin Laden had set in motion. The founder of al Qaeda had awakened the ghosts of *Ikhwān*, the Bedouin warriors and Wahhabi zealots who once rode with Abdulaziz ibn Saud in spreading terror beyond their arid inner sanctum of Najd. When the *Ikhwān* warriors threatened the House of Saud in the making, Abdulaziz ibn Saud had them mowed down with weapons supplied by the British. Years later, like the forgotten *Ikhwān* warriors, the Salafi-Wahhabi jihadists mobilized for holy war by Osama bin Laden pose the most severe threat to the continuing rule of the House of Saud and with it the entire post-WWI order in the Fertile Crescent.

ix.

Loretta Napoleoni, an oil and energy specialist, described ISIS as "the Islamist phoenix". It had arisen from the depredations of the Iraq War and the sectarian conflict inside Syria following the "Arab Spring" uprisings of 2011. The difference between al Qaeda and ISIS was that the former remained a network of *jihādi* warriors and the latter was a state in formation.

Osama bin Laden had spoken about the restoration of the Caliphate, while Mullah Omar of Afghanistan had taken for himself the title of *Amir al-Mu'minīn* ("Commander of the Believers") in the aftermath of the Soviet-Afghan war. But when Abu Bakr al-Baghdadi declared himself the Caliph and announced the rebirth of the Caliphate, he turned the nostalgia of a broad segment of Muslims into a practical reality to defend. As Napoleoni observed, "Though al Baghdadi's men are willing to die for the Caliphate, their dream, by contrast, is positive and contemporary: they want to experience the Caliphate on this earth, not only in the afterlife."[33]

In the escalating struggle over the Fertile Crescent, more than a decade after the 2003 American-led regime change in Iraq, the pertinent question was whether the United States will hold the line between Saudi Arabia and the ISIS-hatched Caliphate, or let that struggle spill over into the kingdom. In the 1920s this line was held by Britain, but after the Second World War Britain was an exhausted power and retreat from her vast overseas empire became an imperative. In the wake of Britain's retreat, the United States took upon itself the burden of maintaining regional order in the Middle East.

In defending the regional order (as shaped by the Sykes-Picot cartography from the Great War) against Saddam Hussein's invasion and occupation of Kuwait, President George H.W. Bush ironically brought into the open the nightmare scenario of what might follow once the tyrant in Baghdad was removed. The horrific uncertainties of post-Saddam Iraq deterred President Bush from sending American forces all the way into Baghdad after they had routed the Iraqi army in Kuwait during the first Gulf War in 1991.

The states of the Fertile Crescent and the Gulf are, as Egyptian diplomat Tahseen Bashir once remarked, "tribes with flags." Iraq was an entity created by Britain, in which Shi'ites and Sunni tribes were expected to share power with the Kurds. It was eventually held together by the Sunni-dominated military and by appeals to Arab nationalism, which was in practical terms a fiction. Sunni Arab Muslims were a minority within an Iraq with a Shi'ite Arab majority, and the Sunni Arab fear of Shi'ite revanchism was fuelled by the awareness of how they had abused Shi'ite Muslims.

There was no mistaking the nature of Saddam Hussein's brutal despotism, and the extent to which his tyranny rested upon the fears of his Sunni clansmen. Soon after the Iraqi army was expelled from Kuwait, Kanan Makiya imagined what could occur if the tyrant was killed or removed:

> After Saddam is gone, when people's lives and those of their loved ones look as if they are on the chopping block, Sunni fears of what the Shi'a might do to them in the name of Islam are going to become the major force of Iraqi politics. The more Iraq's Shi'a assert themselves as Shi'a, the greater will be the tendency of Iraq's Sunni minority to fight to the bitter end before allowing anything that so much as smells of an Islamic republic to be established in Iraq. They see in such a state—whether rightly or wrongly is irrelevant—their own annihilation.[34]

Makiya knew the tribal and sectarian nature of his country, as did the *jihādi* warriors associated with al Qaeda, who moved into Iraq in the wake of regime change in 2003. Their deliberate assault on Shi'ite centers and shrines, masterminded by the ruthless al Qaeda associate in Iraq, Abu Musab al-Zarqawi, was coldly calculated to launch the Sunni-Shi'a war in the Fertile Crescent. It worked. American forces tracked and killed al-Zarqawi in June 2006, but ISIS praised his deeds with remembrance of him as one of its founding fathers.

The Salafi-Wahhabi holy warriors also sensed that the American public would turn against a long and ugly war of attrition in the Middle East, just as it had turned against the war in Vietnam. Under President Obama began America's military disengagement from Iraq, after the American public softened its support for continued military involvement in Iraq and the broader Middle East thereby confirming the expectations of the Salafi-Wahhabi *jihādi* warriors.

Regime change in Baghdad had led to the formation of a Shi'a dominated majority government. What Makiya prophesied after the first Gulf War eventually came about, as Iraqis became trapped in the spiral of sectarian killings. The Sunni-Shi'a schism has been the main divide in Muslim history since the early years of Islam, and in recent years Sunni Arabs in Iraq began to perceive their sectarian interests under siege. The Sunni insurgency in Iraq was fuelled by the desire to restore Sunni pride and identity, and to reverse the slippage of Sunni power.

The rise of ISIS, the Sunni insurgency in Iraq and the Sunni rebellion in Syria against the minority Alawite regime of Bashar al-Assad became linked and, as a result, the frontier between the two states was more or less erased. ISIS disrupted the Iranian arc of influence and power that came out of Tehran and passed through Baghdad and Damascus into Beirut. Although the rise of ISIS might be threatening to the House of Saud's rule in Arabia, doctrinally the two are natural allies in the Sunni-Shi'a conflict, which has the likelihood of escalating into a new version of the Iran-Iraq war of the 1980s. Saudi relations with ISIS were cloaked in mystery; similarly, Saudi relations with al Qaeda, despite the public break with Osama bin Laden before the September 11, 2001 attacks, remain guarded. The Saudis have, moreover, redirected the internal opposition of hardline Wahhabi zealots into support for *jihādi* politics abroad. The Sunni-Shi'a conflict has continued to provide ample opportunity for the Saudis to fund *jihād* and maintain internal support of the hardline Wahhabi ideologues. In keeping with this policy, the Saudis will co-opt remnants of the defeated ISIS in waging *jihād* against Iran and her allies in the Fertile Crescent.

In *Funding Evil,* Rachel Ehrenfeld documented Saudi funding of al Qaeda despite the special relationship between Saudi Arabia and the United States. Given the evidence that the history of the Saudi-Wahhabi alliance in establishing the kingdom is filled with bigotry and terror, Saudi Arabia remains a state devoted to the cause of *jihād* in spreading Wahhabism within the Sunni Muslim world and beyond.

In a report about a leaked briefing on Saudi Arabia by the late scholar Laurent Murawiec, given in July 2002 to a Pentagon advisory committee, the Defense Policy Board, Thomas Ricks of the *Washington Post* reported, "The Saudis are active at every level of the terror chain, from planners to financiers, from cadre to foot-soldier, from ideologist to cheerleader."[35] Murawiec's book on Saudi Arabia, *Princes of Darkness: The Saudi Assault on the West*, published in 2005, was an explosive account of the insidious ways in which the House of Saud has been an incubator of Islamism and has funded the enemies of the United States, such as the various affiliates of the Muslim Brotherhood and the Palestinian Hamas—all the while the House of Saud depended for its own security on American protection. A Pentagon spokeswoman, after the briefing by Murawiec, went on record to state that it did not reflect the official views of the Department of Defense. This swift denial indicated the sensitivity inside Washington on the questionable nature of the American-Saudi relationship, which in the context of September 11, 2001 required the most serious reassessment, and which the American leadership has resisted.

In the circumstances of American military disengagement from Iraq and the investment in time and effort made by President Obama to reach an agreement with Iran, the Saudi rulers likely will support the war ISIS instigated against the Shi'ite population in Iraq and Syria. It was reported in the British press that Prince Bandar bin Sultan, former Saudi ambassador in Washington and former chief of Saudi intelligence, told Sir Richard Dearlove, head of the British MI6, "The time is not far off in the Middle East, Richard, when it will be literally 'God help the Shi'a'. More than a billion Sunnis have simply had enough of them."[36]

ISIS's campaign to consolidate its hold on its captured territories was marked by the deliberate ethnic cleansing of minorities in the region, and destruction of ancient sites and ancient arts stored in regional museums. As V.S. Naipaul noted, "ISIS is dedicated to a contemporary holocaust." The Saudi silence in the face of such crimes against humanity signified acquiescence and tacit embrace of ISIS.

There was method in the genocidal violence perpetrated by ISIS against minority Christians and Yazidis, and the majority

Shi'a Muslims in the region. It was designed to spread fear, to weaken the opposition, and by the force of ideology and terror to reconfigure the Fertile Crescent. As Abu Bakr Naji, an Islamist ideologue, wrote, "One who previously engaged in jihad knows that it is naught but violence, crudeness, terrorism, frightening [others], and massacring."[37] Abdulaziz ibn Saud, at the head of his Bedouin *Ikhwān* warriors, would have heartily agreed with Naji and approved the sweep of terror perpetrated by ISIS.

X.

The war for regime change in Iraq after September 11, 2001, launched by President George W. Bush, cannot be re-litigated or undone. It was waged for reasons well considered at the time, and the expectation that regime change could eventually lead, with American support, to the remaking of Iraq as a functioning democracy, was not entirely unreasonable.

American support in the reconstruction of Germany and Japan after 1945 was crucial. The transformation of imperial and militaristic Japan into a peaceful democracy was testimony of how American support can make for a better world of nation-states. In the Korean Peninsula, American troops have held the line between the North and the South since the end of the Korean War in 1953; this has made the vital difference in turning South Korea into a democracy and an advanced industrial society.

But America itself changed in the intervening decades since the Second World War. The immense burden of securing the post-1945 world order through the Cold War decades and beyond took its toll. The war in Vietnam stretched to its breaking point the public support for indefinite overseas military engagement against hostile populations that seemingly posed no immediate or existential threat to the country. In the Iraq war, such public support for defeating insurgency and terror, for assisting in nation-building, and for keeping secure the post-WWI settlement for the region, eventually got drained.

An American disengagement from the Middle East under President Donald Trump, if this should occur, could set the stage for a reconfiguration of the states in the Fertile Crescent. The broader Sunni-Shi'a war, in which Saudi Arabia as the major Sunni (Wahhabi) Arab power will confront Iran as a potential nuclear power, is the ominous cloud that hangs over the Fertile Crescent and beyond. The potential for other countries and terrorist groups in the region to acquire nuclear weapons could turn the Sunni-Shi'a conflict into an apocalyptic war between Arabs and Persians. A precursor of such a war in a more limited version was the eight-year long Iran-Iraq war of the nineteen-eighties launched by Saddam Hussein to dismantle the Islamic republic established by Ayatollah Khomeini in 1979.

There is another possible scenario, though improbable to imagine under the present circumstances of tumult across the Middle East. The defeat of ISIS followed by its dismantling, as President Trump indicated would be the objective of his administration during the Republican primaries ahead of November 2016 election, would leave Iran as the dominant power in the region, exercising influence across the Fertile Crescent through the Shi'a majority population in Iraq and the Shi'a proxy militias in Syria and Lebanon. Iran then ironically might well become the midwife of Sunni Arab and Israeli partnership.

An acceptance of the Jewish state by Saudi Arabia is not far-fetched if and when the House of Saud, faced with an existential threat from Iran as a potential nuclear power, seeks strategic support from Israel. The Saudi rulers could ask for and likely receive religious support from the *ulema* of Al-Azhar in Cairo, Egypt, on the basis that it is pleasing to Allah that the descendants of Ismail—Abraham's son by Hagar—reconcile with the descendants of Isaac—Abraham's son by Sarah. There is no explicit prohibition of Muslim-Jew relationship in the Qur'an, nor there is any theological basis in Islam of bigotry against Jews referred to in the Qur'an as *ahl al-kitab* or the "people of the Book." It is tribalism that is at the core of Arab and Muslim anti-Jew sentiments turned against Israel. But the politics of tribalism—"the enemy of my enemy is my friend"—is, however amoral and destructive, basically shallow, opportunistic, interest driven and, in this respect, in substance in accordance with the view about politics attributed to the British statesman Lord Palmerston that "Nations have no permanent friends or allies, they only have permanent interests." If this were to occur, ISIS in its death throes will have ironically contributed in bringing together Sunni Muslims and Jews that can only be in balance positive for the future of the Middle East and the Muslim world.

VII.

Islamism in the Rear-View Mirror

It is good to recall that three centuries ago, around the year 1660, two of the greatest monuments of modern times were erected, one in the West and one in the East; St. Paul's Cathedral in London and the Taj Mahal in Agra. Between them the two symbolize, perhaps better than words can describe, the comparative level of architectural technology, the comparative level of affluence and sophistication the two cultures had attained at that epoch of history... [But] about the same time there was also created – and this time only in the West – a third monument, a monument still greater in its eventual import for humanity's future. This was Newton's Principia, *published in 1687. Newton's work had no counterpart in the India of the Moghuls.*

Abdus Salam[1]

We shall have our manhood. We shall have it or the earth will be leveled by our attempts to gain it.

Eldridge Cleaver[2]

A decade after operatives of al Qaeda attacked the United States, the Arab and Muslim world was seized by popular uprisings. The so-called "Arab Spring" erupted in Tunisia, swept into Libya and Egypt where dictators of long standing were toppled and the regime of Bashar al-Assad in Syria was besieged in a bloody standoff against insurgents determined to topple his dictatorship.

It is perhaps too early to state definitively that the "Arab Spring" is the direct consequence—which no one imagined—of hijacked jetliners flown into tall buildings in New York. Eventually, however, the political success of the Muslim Brotherhood movement, and its parties in the Middle East, might be viewed as the fall-out strategically anticipated by Osama bin Laden and his al Qaeda network determined to precipitate a region-wide war. They might even have hoped that the war's twists and turns would destabilize established regimes in the Middle East and North Africa to the advantage of the region's Islamists.

The terrorist attacks on September 11, 2001 did not erupt out of the blue. The nineteen hijackers of the four American jetliners were all Arab Muslims selected by the leadership of al Qaeda, and financed and trained for such an operation. Their mission was an act of war as carefully planned as the attack sixty years earlier on December 7, 1941 by the Japanese imperial navy on Pearl Harbor. The differences between the two acts of aggression were many, but the one striking fact was that the United States in both instances came to be viewed as the enemy to be drawn into war. The varying responses of the government and the people of the United States to these two acts of aggression also indicate how greatly American society changed in the intervening years.

What is of greater interest is that most Americans on that September morning were just as unaware of the intense turmoil raging within the Muslim world in general and the Middle East in particular, as they were unaware in December 1941 of Japanese politics and of the extent to which Japan was already militarily engaged on the Asian mainland.

The renowned Middle East scholar, Bernard Lewis, in "The Roots of Muslim Rage"[3] was possibly the first to point to an increasingly hostile attitude among Muslims in general, and Arabs and Iranians in particular, toward the West and, especially toward the United States. "Muslim rage" was evident in the 1979 Iranian revolution, which brought about the overthrow of the Shah and the monarchy. The Shah had been a loyal ally of the United States in a region endowed with oil resources that gave it immense strategic importance. The revolution, however, under the leadership of aging cleric Ayatollah Ruhollah Khomeini—about whom most Americans, including those in government, knew very little—became Islamic and anti-West.

Also in 1979, there was a siege of Ka'aba, the holy mosque in Mecca. The siege was begun by armed militants from inside Saudi Arabia enraged by the perceived corruption of the Saudi ruling family and Western influence inside the kingdom. The siege of Ka'aba—the holiest site in Islam and the location of the annual Muslim pilgrimage—and the violence that followed, shocked Muslims around the world. Two years later, in October 1981, Egypt's President Anwar Sadat was assassinated while attending a military parade. His murderer was an Egyptian military officer with ties to an extremist wing of the radical Islamic movement in Egypt headed by the Muslim Brotherhood. Part of the reason for Sadat's murder was the peace treaty he had signed with Israel two years earlier.

There were also popular unrest, violence, terrorism and war found in the Middle East and across the Muslim world. The list is long. Independence from European colonial rule had consequences contrary to the expectations of prosperity in an independent future. Unrest among Muslims was also symptomatic of their anger, disillusionment, and frustration with the state of affairs in their native lands. Independence did not bring any substantial improvement to the prevailing social and economic conditions for most people. Instead, the situation deteriorated as the population grew, and, with it, poverty. The promise of freedom and democracy with the end of Europe's colonial rule over Muslims was often belied by what came to be dictatorships in the newly independent Muslim majority states. There were wars—Arab states against Israel, Pakistan against India—with non-Muslim armies repeatedly humiliating the military forces of Muslim countries.

Lewis described with much sympathy the sense of Muslim frustration, or rage, arising from the failure to meet the requirements of modernity the West had pioneered in politics, arts and sciences. He spoke of Islam as "one of the world's great religions," and emphasized that it "has brought comfort and peace of mind to countless millions of men and women." He went on to note that Islam "has given dignity and meaning to drab and impoverished lives. It has taught people of different races to live in brotherhood and people of different creeds to live side by side in reasonable tolerance. It inspired a great civilization in which others besides Muslims lived creative and useful lives and which, by its achievement, enriched the whole world." And yet, Lewis observed, there were periods in Islam's history "when it inspired in some of its followers a mood of hatred and violence. It is our misfortune that part, though by no means all or even most, of the Muslim world is now going through such a period, and that much, though again not all, of that hatred is directed against us."

Such was the situation in Muslim lands entering the final decade of the twentieth century. This rage among Muslims, fuelled by grievances and the sense of past humiliations suffered at the hands of Western powers, turned ominous. Although a Jew and an outsider, Lewis read the pulse of the Muslim world well. He was not alone. Muslim thinkers had also reflected on the condition of their culture and civilization and the extent of Muslim backwardness relative to the non-Muslim West. The disparity between the West on one side, and Islam or the Muslim world on the other, was so vast that it raised questions as to whether the Muslim world had become moribund, decrepit and, more specifically, whether Muslims might have to jettison their culture in order to embrace modernity and follow the West.

In the early years of the twentieth century, before the First World War had turned Europe into a killing field, Muhammad Iqbal (1876-1938) spoke in verses of immense power, beauty and passion about the malaise of the Muslim world. Iqbal, revered as the poet-philosopher of Pakistan, was of Indian birth, and wrote his poetry in Urdu and Persian. In his controversial, yet frequently cited, two long poems, *Shikwa* ("Complaint") and *Jawab-i-Shikwa* ("Answer to the Complaint"),[4] Iqbal discussed the failure of Muslims to maintain the dynamism of Islam and its civilizational values. In "Answer," Iqbal made God respond derisively to Muslims who complained of being ignored and forgotten despite their fidelity in good and bad times. God, in Iqbal's stirring verses, reminded Muslims that they succeeded when they were dynamic in thought and action: when they were bold, took risks and were creative.

Iqbal was not alone in advocating reform and re-awakening Islamic civilization from its stupor. Iqbal admired Mustafa Kemal Atatürk, the founder of the modern Turkish Republic in the aftermath of the First World War. Kemal was an ardent modernizer and an enthusiast in adopting Western values in culture and politics. He abolished religious rule based on Sharia law.

There were others, such as Malek Bennabi (1905-73), an Algerian born in Constantine and educated in Paris. Bennabi reflected upon the possible causes for the decay of Islam as a civilization and concluded, as had Iqbal, that the loss of internal dynamism and critical thought had impoverished Muslims. He conceived of history in cyclical terms according to Ibn Khaldun, the immensely influential 14th century thinker from Tunis: birth of civilization, followed by growth, expansion, contraction, loss of movement, then demise. Bennabi commented that the Islamic civilization, once the Qur'anic pressure at its beginning "deadened, little by little the Muslim world came to a stop like a motor that had consumed its last litre of petrol."[5]

During the first half of the twentieth century, the views of modernist Muslim thinkers, such as Iqbal and Bennabi, were ascendant within the Muslim world. Again according to Lewis, "At first the Muslim response to Western civilization was one of admiration and emulation—an immense respect for the achievements of the West, and a desire to imitate and adopt them."[6]

But an alternative view emerged among Muslims that rejected the West and all of its cultural and political values. This alternative view hearkened back to an idealized picture of the first century of Islam (7th-8th century C.E.), when the Arab-

Islamic Empire was in the making and Arab rulers laid down the template of Islamic civilization. It viewed the West as an implacable enemy of Islam and Muslims, and it set its goals in driving Western powers out of Muslim lands and bringing to an end Western influence among Muslims. It spoke about the necessity of *jihād* (holy war) to achieve its goal of returning Muslim lands to the rule of Shariah. And it declared *jihād* to be one of the central pillars of Islam—contrary to the traditional consensus of religious scholars. This view was the seed of what grew into Islamism, a twentieth century political ideology that drew exclusively upon that strain of violence, sectarianism, and religious supremacism that have riddled historical Islam.

In the middle years of the last century, at the end of colonialism in Muslim lands,[7] there was an effort to bring about rapid modernization through the adoption of Western ideas. There was keen interest in building heavy industries, constructing dams and hydroelectric projects, encouraging urbanization, expanding communication networks, investing in higher education, encouraging female education and women in professions, and raising modern armies. But these efforts were not accompanied by an equally urgent commitment of the ruling elites for democracy. Modernization in effect became imitative of the West with little understanding on the part of the modernizing elite of the importance of the political culture of modern West. Muslims in general had no understanding of what democracy meant, and the idea of freedom was more or less non-existent in Muslim experience. As the Syrian poet and literary critic Ali Ahmed Said `Isbar, known widely by his pseudonym Adonis, observed:

> Let us not forget that equality and democracy do not emanate from the Qur'anic text or from Arab history. Democracy comes from the West. Today we talk about freedom. But freedom is a notion that doesn't exist in the Text or in the Islamic context. Freedom, and democracy, are notions that were created in the West; they were forged by Western thought.[8]

This basic lack of a fuller understanding of modernization by the modernizing elite of the post-colonial Muslim societies left them vulnerable to the ideological opposition mounted by Islamists against modernity—the political culture of modern democracy based on ideas of freedom and equality—being not merely un-Islamic but, more damningly, anti-Islamic. And when the collision came between the proponents of modernization and the Islamist opponents, as a result of the negative effects of modernization dislocating traditional societies, the Islamists gradually gained the upper hand over the modernizing elite.

In explaining the reversal of Muslim reformers and modernizers, Lewis again observed, "For vast numbers of Middle Easterners, Western-style economic methods brought poverty, Western-style political institutions brought tyranny, even Western-style warfare brought defeat. It is hardly surprising that so many were willing to listen to voices telling them that the old Islamic ways were best and that their only salvation was to throw aside the pagan innovations of the reformers and return to the True Path that God had prescribed for his people."[9]

V.S. Naipaul, the celebrated writer awarded the 2001 Nobel Prize for Literature, published in 1981 an account of his travels in Muslim lands. Naipaul's *Among the Believers* was an eyewitness report of the Muslim world in turmoil. His journey took him to Tehran in the midst of a crisis, when Iranian students, following the radical Islamist prescriptions of Ayatollah Khomeini's sermonizing, took fifty-two Americans at the U.S. embassy as hostages and held them for over a year. Naipaul described the situation as if "the Muslim world had been on the boil."[10]

As the 1979 Iranian revolution became a tipping point for the Muslim world, Islamist opponents of Western-style modernization seized the political initiative while Muslim reformers began to lose ground and turned defensive. In 1971, Pakistan, then the most populous Muslim state, broke apart as a result of a bloody civil conflict and a self-destructive war with India. This

Muslim-on-Muslim violence in effect turned genocidal, with massacres in Bangladesh by the Pakistani army, after the people of Bangladesh (then East Pakistan) had voted in a national election for a secular, democratic government; the generals rejected the election results that ignited popular civil unrest followed by military brutalities.

In the following decades violence inside the Muslim world became commonplace. Modernization came to be viewed disparagingly, and the modernizers were blamed for the wretched situation of Muslims. The "Muslim rage" insisted, instead, on a return to the past.

This newly acquired consensus was reflected in the Cairo Declaration of August 5, 1990, released by the foreign ministers of the member states of the Organization of Islamic Co-operation (OIC). Evidently intended as a response to the United Nations' Declaration of Human Rights of 1948, the Cairo Declaration stipulated that all rights and freedoms for Muslims were derived from Shariah. It declared, "Shariah is the only source of reference for the explanation or clarification to any of the articles of this Declaration." This signified the long and dispiriting retreat of modernizers who, like Muhammad Iqbal, had greeted with enthusiasm the creation of the Turkish Republic by Mustafa Kemal some seventy years earlier.

By the time the second millennium drew to an end, the internal unrest in the Muslim world had reached a breaking point. The decade long war between Saddam Hussein's Iraq and Khomeini's Iran in the 1980s displayed the ferocity inherent in past sectarian conflicts within the Muslim world. The Arab states were divided over how to confront Israel once Egypt had made peace with the Jewish state. The Russian invasion of Afghanistan in 1979, and the long war ignited by the invasion aroused Islamic sentiments. Ironically, in this instance, Muslim "rage" was harnessed by the United States to deliver a punishing defeat to the Soviet Union's imperial overreach.

Moscow's admission of defeat and the Soviet withdrawal from Afghanistan emboldened militant Muslims, who insisted their *jihād* had defeated a military superpower. These Muslim warriors took the message of the Muslim Brotherhood and the Jamaat-i-Islami—Islam is *jihād* and *jihād* is obligatory on Muslims—to its logical extreme. Like the Bolsheviks in 1917, al Qaeda's *jihādis* were revolutionaries in a hurry. They wanted to push history on their terms. They argued that confrontation with the West and its most powerful representative, the United States, was inevitable, and they planned to precipitate it. A return to "authentic" Islam, to a time and place before the West and its corrupt ways had contaminated the Arab cradle of Islam, required *jihād*. Accordingly, al-Qaeda developed as a network of militant Muslims in a political climate of spreading Muslim rage. Driven by its utopian view of an Islamic society, al-Qaeda and its supporters prepared for an asymmetrical war waged through indiscriminate terrorism against the West by Islamic warriors of Allah.

The collapse of the Soviet Union caught the West by surprise. Some saw the end of the Cold War as the end of history. After the long, demanding and exhaustive effort that went into the containment of Soviet Communism, Americans turned inwards. Few in the West paid serious attention to the troubles brewing inside the Muslim world, and which were headed for an explosion.

September 11, 2001 was a return to history with a vengeance. And terrorism in the name of Islam exposed a civilization's internal rot as it wrestled with its own demise.

The modern world, which many Muslims dislike and oppose, cannot be "un-invented." Despite their rage, Muslims face a challenge in a new century that is essentially the same as the one described by Iqbal at the beginning of the twentieth century. It is also somewhat similar to the one Christians and Christendom confronted over five hundred years ago. This challenge consists in determining how to maintain faith in the context of the revolutionary advances in philosophy and science. Christianity met the challenge at the dawn of a new age, which came to be defined as the Enlightenment, by separating the realms of faith and politics. Once the Muslim world has overcome its rage, it would do well to draw on the experience of Christianity in accommodating modernity.

The Muslim world cannot remain in a boil indefinitely. There is no ready answer to how a civilization can be repaired, or if one master cure is available for the remedy of a broken civilization. Yet Muslims need to find a way of adapting their customs, values and beliefs to the requirements of the modern world, and this will be their burden for much of the twenty-first century.

The West, however, cannot stand apart at a distance while the Muslim world confronts its problems. As the West did in its relationship with the Soviet Union during the Cold War, it needs to work out a prudent, safe and firm set of policies for its relationship with the Muslim world in the years ahead. As Muslims in rage fail to stop their descent into an inferno of their own making, the West is inevitably and unavoidably drawn into the troubles of the Muslim world.

ii.

Two authors—Britain's Marxist historian, Eric Hobsbawm, and American historian, John Lukacs—placed the twentieth century in brackets between the outbreak of World War I and the collapse of the Soviet Union.[11] In contrast, the nineteenth century was the age of European powers. Britain, as the pre-eminent power, ruled the seas across continents. The two world wars of the twentieth century might be seen in retrospect as one massive terminal conflagration of the European powers. The age of Europe came to an end in 1945 with the continent divided, the United States and the Soviet Union locked in a contest for supremacy, and the colonial possessions of European powers in Asia and Africa acquiring independence.

In this view of history, the Bolshevik, or Communist, Revolution of October 1917 in Russia was as much a pivotal event as was the outbreak of World War I. The war exposed Czarist Russia as the weakest link in the European capitalist system and allowed for communist agitations against the Czar's rule eventually to succeed. The emergence of the Soviet Union as a communist power was a threat to the liberal democratic political order based on capitalist economics. But the Soviet Union was overshadowed during the first half of the twentieth century despite the threat it posed to Europe by the rise and success of National Socialism, or Nazism, in Germany under Hitler. The deranged German dictator brought Europe to ruin, and set the stage for the Cold War between the United States and the Soviet Union. That conflict ended only when the Soviet Union collapsed nearly five decades later.

The grand strategic objective of the United States during the Cold War years was to contain any further expansion of the Soviet Union beyond the gains made by Moscow during World War II. Called the "containment policy," it drew a line running parallel along the frontier of the Soviet client states in Europe and Asia. The real or perceived threats of Soviet expansion beyond this line required an adequate response of the West. That strategy took America into wars in the Korean peninsula, Vietnam, proxy wars in Africa and Central America, and the Cuban Missile crisis. The last terminal confrontation between the two superpowers occurred in Afghanistan, when the Soviet Union sent troops in support of its Afghan allies in Kabul, and Washington armed the Afghan resistance with the help of Saudi Arabia and Pakistan.

The Cold War years also affected the domestic and foreign politics of Muslims countries. The states of the Middle East and the Persian Gulf, located on the southern perimeter of the Soviet Union and at great distance from the United States, possess an abundance of easily accessible fossil fuels—by some estimates, more than two-thirds of the world's known reserves.

Next to a divided Europe, this was the region most vulnerable to Soviet penetration, and the most strategically important to the interests of the West. The West had a long, troubling history of relations with the people of the region, and with their religion and culture. But the shadow of the Soviet Union falling over the region required the United States to paper over differences and likely difficulties between Washington and Muslim-majority states located in the region on either sides of the Persian Gulf, while bringing them close through defense arrangements. It meant looking at the politics of this region through the prism of security concerns: of "giving a pass" to the rulers of these countries for violations of human rights and suppression of democratic demands. In particular, it meant overlooking almost any unacceptable behaviour by whoever possessed oil reserves, so long as they pledged to co-operate with the United States in securing vital interests of the West in the region.

The political and military leadership in Washington and other Western capitals seemed to have concluded early in the Cold War that the religion and cultural traditions of the people in the region—Islam and Muslims—were intrinsically hostile to godless communism and would, therefore, be natural allies of the West against the Soviet Union and Communism. This view went mostly uncontested, and it served well the converging interests of the Western powers and the political rulers in Muslim countries who supported the political *status quo,* both domestically and in terms of regional stability.

If our knowledge of the world and its usefulness is generally conditioned by our needs, our needs might well be unlimited, but our resources are finite and our knowledge incomplete. During the decades of the Cold War, the knowledge of both superpowers and regional actors about each other, about the situation at hand and what it meant in terms of their respective needs, and about the unintended consequences of their choices and actions, were warped by the logic of the Cold War itself.

The relationship between the modern West and the Muslim world is inherently unequal. The modern West is the progeny of Christendom with its own distinct history of borrowings and influences from ancient Greece, the Romans, the Jews, and the political thinkers of Europe. The Muslim world, although near Europe, has always viewed itself as a civilization distinct and separate from the West. The history of these two civilizations has been one riddled with rivalry, conflicts, suspicions and claims of wrongs done against one another. The Cold War only tentatively masked this history; once the Cold War ended, the troubled past of the two unequal civilizations, historically at odds, was bound to re-surface.

The Cold War, however, as it played out through the twentieth century, distorted the images that the West and the Muslim world held of each other. The West—liberal, democratic and secular—came to see the rest of the world gradually adopting its values, consistent with the idea of progress in history. The collapse of the Soviet Union lent support to the view that the ideals defining the West were indeed universal and, notwithstanding differences among cultures, that the world was headed towards globalization under the tutelage of the West.

This optimism was reflected, for instance, in Francis Fukuyama's *The End of History and the Last Man,* published after the collapse of the Soviet Union, and with it the discrediting of Communism as an ideology. Fukuyama pointed out that the world's most developed countries were also successful democracies and liberal societies. The future in the new century, without ideological rivalry among great powers, looked promising, as competing ideologies had only generated conflicts in the world. "A world made up of liberal democracies, then, should have much less incentive for war," wrote Fukuyama, "since all nations would reciprocally recognize one another's legitimacy."[12]

In the midst of the optimism prevailing at the end of the Cold War, although such optimism was not shared by all in the West, there was little apprehension about people in non-Western cultures reading differently the meaning or lesson of contemporary history. There were troubles in the world during the decade after the Berlin Wall was taken down in 1989—local conflicts in the Balkans and the disintegration of Yugoslavia into its constituent parts based on ethnic and religious identities; conflicts generated by failed states, as in Somalia, Rwanda and Sudan; war over Kuwait and its aftermath as Saddam Hussein's Iraq, a disaffected power, threatened its neighbours; tribal conflicts in Afghanistan, as the Taliban consolidated their hold on Kabul and the rest of the country; Palestinian unrest; Arab grievances; Israeli insecurity; India and Pakistan acquiring nuclear weapons; nuclear threats in the Far East from North Korea; and the rise of China and India as emerging powers in a new century—but these were all considered as manageable within the rubric of the United Nations' authority and "great power" diplomacy.

The preoccupation with the Cold War made political leaders and policy advisors in Washington and other Western capitals fail to assess properly the long-term threats of the Muslim world "on the boil," in V.S. Naipaul's apt description. The politicization of Islam and its effects on the social order of the Muslim world were not given proper scrutiny. The turn of events leading up to September 11, 2001 and its aftermath therefore came as a shock. The passage of time since September 11 has worn off considerably this shock, yet the West remains unsure of what is to be done to contain—if not defeat—radical Muslims, or Islamists, as they gain in influence and power.

The West, however, cannot remain in denial of, or aloof from, the threat that politicized Islam, or Islamism, poses to Western interests in the Muslim world, as well as to those Muslims who want economic development, democracy and peace for their societies. Regardless of how the United States, either alone or leading the West, will remain involved with the Muslim world,

Islamism demands attention and an adequate response ideologically and militarily, well into the twenty-first century, just as Communism and the Soviet Union did in the twentieth century.

iii.

The unlimited and proliferating problems in our world are commonly considered technical in nature, and their solutions primarily technical as well: a modernization made of machines and computers. But if September 11, 2001 bears any significance beyond the idea of rage taking hold of a people and impelling them into monstrous acts of terror, then surely it tells us to beware of reducing our problems to merely technical matters. We do not inhabit a soulless world. Man, by nature, is as driven by a yearning of the soul, however misguided at times this might be, as he is by material needs and utilitarian calculations.

Irving Babbitt, a literary critic and a leading thinker of new humanism at Harvard during the early decades of the twentieth century, in his introduction to *Democracy and Leadership* wrote,

> According to Mr. Lloyd George, the future will be even more exclusively taken up than is the present with the economic problem, especially with the relations between capital and labor. In that case, one is tempted to reply, the future will be very superficial. When studied with any degree of thoroughness, the economic problem will be found to run into the political problem, the political problem in turn into the philosophical problem, and the philosophical problem itself to be almost indissolubly bound up at last with the religious problem.[13]

Babbitt's words are a reminder that ultimately man does "not live by bread alone," that his rage is likely greatest when he senses the vision he cherishes about his world has gone awry, or is broken, or abused. At such times he will neither be consoled nor restrained from taking extreme measures to set right what he, even mistakenly, believes has turned wrong.

The Muslim world is broken and, ultimately, the problem for Muslims in repairing their world is a religious problem. If their belief is at odds with the world they inhabit, then their belief has to be reformed, for the world cannot forcefully be made to conform to their belief.

The Muslim world is not monolithic; it is hugely diverse. There are competing views among Muslims on how they view Islam as their faith—as a matter of personal belief, or as a belief packaged in the form of an ideology. Broadly speaking, the struggle within Islam in our time—in which September 11, 2001, London's July 7, 2005 suicide-bombing of the transport system, the Madrid train bombings, ISIS's beheadings, and the list of atrocities has gotten longer—is between Muslims who embrace the values of the modern world in terms of freedom, individual rights, gender equality and democracy on the one side and Muslims opposing these values and insisting on adherence to the Shariah-based legal system on the other. This struggle, therefore, goes to the very heart of how Muslims understand Islam: either as a personal faith and matter of tradition, or as a total system of belief and practice that is antithetical to the norms of the modern world. For Muslims who embrace modernity, Islam is a matter of personal belief, not a political system; Muslims opposed to modernity view Islam ideologically, as *Islamism*, and accordingly they embrace the views of Maududi and Hasan al-Banna, Sayyed Qutb and Khomeini, in which Islam is a totalitarian value-system.

The seeds of this struggle—or, more appropriately, the basis of conceiving of Islam ideologically, and in terms of politics and power—can be traced back to the earliest years of Islam and Muslim history. In recent years, however, beginning in the middle of the twentieth century, Muslims have been compelled to face the challenges of modernity, when, after European colonial rule, Muslim societies became independent. Beyond the few states of the Middle East possessing petro-wealth, Muslim states are almost without exception poor and underdeveloped, and relatively backward culturally, politically and technologically. Muslims, in general, have been denied freedom by those holding power, and have very little experience of liberty as individual freedom.

Hence we have an Islam conceived of by *Islamists* as a totalitarian value system, a political instrument of power and authority, "unchanging," "authentic," and "authoritative", and any Muslim who even questions this version of "Islam" is referred to as a heretic or, worse, an apostate condemned to death.

Muslims opposed to Islamism reject the Islamist view that Islam is unchanging, that the Qur'an is a closed book and not open to interpretation other than the Islamist version that was crafted during the early centuries of Islam and turned authoritative by those in power. Muslims opposing Islamism are in many, if not all, instances, anti-Shariah, and opposed to the political parties or movements associated with Maududi (the Jamaat-i-Islami in South Asia), with Hasan al-Banna and Sayyed Qutb (the Muslim Brotherhood in the countries of the Middle East and North Africa), with Khomeinism (the Shi'a version of Islamism in Iran and among Shi'a Muslims in the Middle East and elsewhere), and with the Wahhabi-Salafi version of Islamism espoused and propagated by the Saudi and Gulf Arabs with their petrodollars.

This struggle between Islamism and Islam—between Islamist Muslims and anti-Islamist Muslims—is the core struggle among Muslims in the world of post-September 11, 2001. Given the vast diversity inside the Muslim world, this core struggle takes many different forms. It also embodies the much-postponed movement for the reform of Islam and the Muslim world, analogous in many ways to the long and complex conflicts waged within Christendom and spread over several centuries through the Reformation, the Counter-Reformation and the accompanying conflicts that spilled over into the modern world.

From a longer historical perspective, this struggle within Islam is unavoidable and necessary, as Muslims individually and collectively strive to reconcile their faith with modernity. It might even be said that the terrorist attacks of September 11, 2001 exposed the simmering, at times violent, tensions within the Muslim world, and propelled the internal conflicts to burst open and remind us once again that the struggle for reform is often inseparable from violence.

The intensity of the struggle between Islam and Islamism can be assessed by the degree of Muslim-on-Muslim violence. The eventual outcome of this struggle can have salutary effects for Muslims and non-Muslims in our interdependent world. But a reformed Islam, which embraces the modern values of science, freedom and democracy, cannot succeed without the support of non-Muslims in a world where no culture or civilization stands in isolation from any other. Hence there is a need for an increased scrutiny within the West of Islam and Muslims. It was missing during the Cold War years, and it is a necessary, positive, spur for the reform of Islam, and for it to be reconciled with modernity and democracy in Muslim countries.

Islam is the last of the great world religions that has remained resistant to modernist reform. It might be said that Islamists turned Islam as *Islamism* into an oppositional force against modernization and modernity. How the Muslim world will eventually become reconciled with modernity might not yet be fully understood, yet an eventual reconciliation despite Islamist opposition cannot be denied indefinitely.

Modernization might be resisted and delayed, as Islamists remain determined to impede it, but it is ultimately irresistible. Its benefits are greatly desired and sought after by swelling numbers of Muslims. In time, historians will note that the brutal conflicts that followed September 11, 2001 were the last desperate failed attempts on the part of those Muslims bent upon restoring a civilization—mistakenly identified as the embodiment of their faith—that was comatose, if not dead.

VIII.

An Afterword

Thou hypocrite, first cast out the beam out of thine own eye; and then shalt thou see clearly to cast out the mote out of thy brother's eye.

The New Testament, St. Matthew, 7:5.

God changes not what is in a people, until they change what is in themselves.

The Qur'an, 13:11.

The two masked men who stormed the Paris office of *Charlie Hebdo* on January 7, 2015 were brothers Saïd Kouachi and Chérif Kouachi. They were in their early thirties born of Algerian parents in Paris, France, and more or less abandoned to the vagaries of life in poverty. From the shadowy under-class world of low crimes to the certainties of *jihād* as a soldier of Allah is the allure of Islamism for those, such as the Kouachi brothers, searching for some purpose in life. Their numbers will keep growing as Islamism grows, as was once with the phenomena of Communism and Nazism.

The massacre at *Charlie Hebdo*—irrespective of whether the cartoons were insulting to some or all Muslims, or how Muslim sensitivities relating to their religion should be accommodated within a secular culture—was not an isolated event. Since Khomeini, the Iranian religious leader, pronounced in 1989 the death sentence on Salman Rushdie for his novel, *The Satanic Verses*, a significant segment of the Muslim world has been ideologically mobilized to a state of war against the West. The religio-cultural dimension of this war is imposition of Islamist categories of permissible (*halal*) and forbidden (*haram*) based on Shariah on

Muslims and non-Muslims alike. As Khomeini reputedly said, the Islamic revolution in Iran was not about the price of watermelon. Such simplistic, yet horrific, answer of Islamists, as cure for the grand failure of economic development in the post-colonial Muslim countries, radicalized Muslim youths without work and facing a dim future.

The Kouachi brothers typically represented the cohorts among the alienated and angry young Muslims born or raised in the West and who, like the disgruntled legions of young in the Muslim world, are readily tempted by the siren-call of Islamists to join the ranks of jihadists in the global *jihād* against modernity. They have become, in the words of the Lebanese-American academic and writer Fouad Ajami, "Islam's Nowhere Men."

The "Nowhere Men" of the Muslim world in the early decades of the twenty-first century turned Islam into a matter of identity and with it followed politics based on the notion of redemptive identity against real or imagined oppressors. This twist of Islam into Islamist identity politics was imitative of Frantz Fanon turning "blackness" into identity politics for Africans in *Black Skin, White Masks,* as they launched their struggle against European colonialism in the second half of the twentieth century. Redemptive identity empowers those who believe they have been treated unjustly in history, and provides them with justification to make the world around them tremble in apprehension of the violence with which they can explode at any time and anywhere.

These "Nowhere Men" of Islam are rootless horde of young Muslim men—sometime with women in their ranks, such as Aafia Siddiqui of Pakistani origin extradited to the United States from Afghanistan in 2008 for her role with al Qaeda; or publicly advocating their identity politics like the Palestinian-American activist Linda Sarsour—who abjure the country of their birth or the country of their origin and swear fealty to the ideology of Islamism, to the cult of *jihād,* to Islam as identity, and are drawn to violence in the cause of establishing a Shariah-based society.

The nineteen jihadists of al Qaeda seizing control of four American jetliners on September 11, 2001 and crashing them into the World Trade Center in New York City and the Pentagon building in Washington typified the phenomenon of "Islam's Nowhere Men" that now haunts the West as much as the Muslim world. They are everywhere. The list of mass killers and suicide bombers from their ranks is long, and getting longer.

We might note from this growing list of "Islam's Nowhere Men" just a few, such as Faisal Shahzad of Pakistani origin residing in New York arrested on May 3, 2010 and convicted on being identified by surveillance camera as the would-be Times Square bomber; Mohammed Bouyeri of Moroccan origin who shot to death Theo van Gogh, a Dutch film-maker, on November 2, 2004 in Amsterdam; the killers of the deadly attacks carried out on November 13, 2015 in Paris who were all young men of North African origin born in France and Belgium, as were Salah Abdesslam and the suspected ringleader Abdelhamid Abaaoud shot dead in a police manhunt for the killers; three of the four suicide bombers of the coordinated attacks on the users of the transport system in London on July 7, 2005—Mohammad Siddique Khan, aged 30; Shehzad Tanveer, aged 22; and Hasib Hussain, aged 18—were of Pakistani origin and British nationals; Major Nidal Hasan, a Palestinian-American, convicted of mass shooting on November 5, 2009 in Fort Hood, Texas; Syed Rizwan Farook and Tashfeen Malik of Pakistani origin residing in the United States were the husband-wife team of killers in the mass shooting in San Bernardino, California on December 2, 2015; Salman Abedi, aged 22, of Libyan origin was the suicide bomber in the mass killing in Manchester, England, on May 22, 2017; Michael Zehaf-Bibeau born to a Libyan father and a French-Canadian mother was the gun-toting intruder into the halls of the Parliament in Ottawa, Canada, on October 22, 2014 after he had killed a member of the Ceremonial Guards at the Ottawa War Memorial; the Tsarnaev brothers, Tamerlan and Dzokhar, of

Chechen origin who carried out the bombings on April 15, 2013 at the Boston marathon; and Mohamed Lahouaiej Bouhlel, a Tunisian, who plowed his delivery truck into a holiday crowd killing dozens celebrating Bastille Day July 14, 2016 in Nice, France.

According to Ajami, these young "Nowhere Men" of Islam are deadly combatants in the Islamist war against modernity. He remarked,

> "A Muslim has no nationality except his belief," the intellectual godfather of the Islamists, Egyptian Sayyid Qutb, wrote decades ago. Qutb's "children" are everywhere now; they carry the nationalities of foreign lands and plot against them. The Pakistani born Faisal Shahzad is a devotee of Sayyid Qutb's doctrine, and Maj. Nidal Hasan, the Fort Hood shooter, was another.
> ...
> Nowadays the Islamic faith is portable. It is carried by itinerant preachers and imams who transmit its teachings to all corners of the world, and from the safety and plenty of the West they often agitate against the very economic and moral order that sustains them. Satellite television plays its part in this new agitation, and the Islam of the tele-preachers is invariably one of damnation and fire. From tranquil, banal places (Dubai and Qatar), satellite television offers an incendiary version of the faith to younger immigrants unsettled by a modern civilization they can neither master nor reject.[1]

The grievances igniting anger and violence among "Islam's Nowhere Men" reflect the numerous problems of failed states of the Muslim world. These have reached a critical mass for which there are no quick, easy, short-term solutions. Wars within Islam over the past half-century have greatly worsened the problems of available resources, human ecology and security. And the rapidly increasing demographic bulge of the youth population across the Middle East and North Africa (MENA) has accelerated the downward spiral of an already broken civilization.

The *Arab Human Development Report 2016* prepared under the banner of the United Nations Development Programme is devoted to the subject of "youth and the prospects for human development in a changing reality." The demographic explosion across the region reflected in the youth bulge makes for a grim future for a people dwarfed by the accumulated problems of the past. The *Report* takes the year 2011 as the beginning of a long-awaited change in the politics of the region when the regimes of strongmen or dictators, as in Tunisia followed by Egypt and Libya, fell. The dramatic upheavals in North Africa rolled over into Syria igniting war across the Fertile Crescent, as the Syrian dictator Bashar al-Asad fought to save his regime with support from Iran and the Russian Federation. The social unrest and uprisings beginning in 2011 were called the "Arab Spring", and though what followed became a nightmare the label stuck. According to the *Report*,

> The protests that took place across several countries and began spreading in 2011 underline the significance of the Arab region's youthful demographic profile. Never before has the region had such a large share of youth; **youth of ages 15-29 make up around 30 percent of the population, or some 105 million people**. Rapid population growth has placed massive pressures on societies and the entire infrastructure of Arab States. It is youth who often translate broader social problems into an explosive and radicalizing mixture (emphasis added).[2]

The youth bulge will grow with the rate of population growth in the region. In 2050 the population is estimated to increase from 350 million in 2010 to 604 million, of which the youth population will likely be somewhere around 150 million. Since development programs in the region hobbled by conflicts will probably be insufficient in providing basic needs for youth, their frustration will grow and with it continued unrest and violence.

A part of the problem now plaguing the MENA countries has been exported by design of the failing authorities, or as a result of the unintended consequences of conditions prevalent in the region. Europe, wittingly or not, has imported the problems of MENA and the Muslim world as a result of the mass migration that accompanied the social unrest of 2011 and after. The spike of terrorist violence in Europe since the Madrid train bombing of March 2004 by "Islam's Nowhere Men," which resulted in 191 deaths and over 1,800 injured was an indicator that problems of the Muslim world and Islamism had gone global.

Fifty years ago the British parliamentarian Enoch Powell speaking at a Conservative party meeting in Birmingham on April 20, 1968 warned of the consequences of open door immigration into Britain. Powell's remarks ended his illustrious political career. A few years later in 1973 Jean Raspail, a French travel writer, published *Le Camp des Saints*, a dystopian work of fiction. An English version of Raspail's fiction, *The Camp of the Saints*, was published in the United States in 1975. Raspail narrated an imagined story of an unusual invasion of Europe by "third world" migrants packed in a barely floating armada of ships set sail from Calcutta, India, then joined by other ships similarly packed with migrants as the armada went around the southern tip of Africa and headed north toward France. It was a bleak story denounced as a work of fiction by an individual unsettled by racist inclinations. Truth, as is often said, is stranger than fiction. Both Powell and Raspail nearly half-century later seem to have been prophetic in their warnings and imaginings.

The Mediterranean as the "Sea of Abraham" was a body of water that separated Europe from MENA. It has become in recent years the bridgehead of migrants from MENA into Europe, and the making of history that might be left best to imaginings. The problems of the Muslim world are now as much the problems of Europe and the West. How these are dealt with will be more or less the immense challenge of the twenty-first century for what was once Christendom, now the West, and what still is Islamdom or *Dār al-Islam* and how together, irrespective of what divides them, they seek remedy for the common malady, Islamism, carried by "Islam's Nowhere Men" across frontiers that afflicts both indiscriminately.

Notes

Preface and Acknowledgements

1. Maxime Rodinson, *Europe and the Mystique of Islam*. Translated from the French by Roger Veinus (Seattle, WA: University of Washington Press, 1987), p. 3.

2. Adonis, *Sufism and Surrealism*. Translated from the Arabic by Judith Cumberbatch (London: Saqi Books, 2016), p. 44 (*italics* added).

Introduction

1. Bernard Lewis, *What Went Wrong? Western Impact and Middle Eastern Response* (New York: Oxford University Press, 2002), p. 3 and p. 6.

2. Marshall G.S. Hodgson, *Rethinking World History: Essays on Europe, Islam, and World History* (New York: Cambridge University Press, 1993), p. 97 and p. 125.

3. See Adonis, *Violence & Islam: Conversations with Houria Abdelouahed* (Cambridge, UK: Polity Press, 2016), p. vii.

4. Quoted by Annemarie Schimmel in *Islam: An Introduction* (Albany, NY: State University of New York Press, 1992), p. v.

5. See Wilferd Madelung, *The succession to Muhammad: A study of the early Caliphate* (Cambridge: Cambridge University Press, 1997).

6. Bertrand Russell, *History of Western Philosophy* (London: George Allen and Unwin Ltd., 1946), p. 10.

I. Islam and Islamism

1. Frithjof Schuon, *Understanding Islam* (Bloomington, IN: World Wisdom Books, Inc., 1994), p. 52.

2. Albert J. Bergesen (editor), *The Sayyid Qutb Reader* (New York: Routledge, 2008), p. 59.

3. S. Abul A'la Maududi, *Islamic Law and Constitution* (Lahore: Islamic Publications Ltd., 1983), p. 146.

4. A. Camus, *The Rebel: An Essay on Man in Revolt* (New York: Vintage Books, 1956), p. 302.

II. On the Historical Muhammad

1. J.D. Crossan, *Jesus: A Revolutionary Biography* (New York: HarperCollins, 1994), p. x.

2. J. Burckhardt, *Reflections on History* (Indianapolis: Liberty Classics, 1979), pp. 271-272.

3. C. Bennett, *In Search of Muhammad* (London and New York: Cassell, 1998), p. 6.

4. T. Khalidi, *Images of Muhammad: Narratives of the Prophet in Islam Across the Centuries* (New York: Doubleday, 2009), p. 297.

5. Ibid., p. 17.

6. Ibid., pp. 1-2.

7. Ibid., p. 18.

8. Ibid., p. 255.

9. Ibn Khaldun, *The Muqadimmah*. Translated from the Arabic by Franz Rosenthal. Edited and Abridged by N.J. Dawood (Princeton, NJ: Princeton University Press Bollingen Series, 1967), p. 11.

10. Ibid., p. 35.

11. Ibid., p. 36.

12. Bennett, p. 32.

13. Khalidi, p. 291.

14. A. Dashti, *Twenty Three Years: A Study of the Prophetic Career of Mohammad* (London: George Allen & Unwin, 1985), p. 21.

15. Khalidi, p. 296.

16. M. Lings, *Muhammad: his life based on the earliest sources* (Rochester, Vermont: Inner Traditions, 1983), p. 300.

17. See M.H. Hart, *The 100: A Ranking of the Most Influential Persons in History* (New York: Citadel Press, 1989).

18. M. Rodinson, *Mohammed* (Harmondsworth, England: Penguin Books Ltd, 1971), pp. 312-313.

19. J. Kirsch, *King David: The Real Life of the Man Who Ruled Israel* (New York: Ballantine Books, 2000) p. 2.

20. A.J. Heschel, *God In Search Of Man* (New York: The Noonday Press, 1983) p. 136.

21. T.S. Eliot, "The Hollow Man." *Collected Poems* (London: Faber and Faber, 1963).

22. Rodinson, *Mohammed*, p. 313.

III. On the Historical Qur'an

1. B. Pascal, *The Pensées*. A New Translation by J.M. Cohen (Harmondsworth, UK: Penguin Books, 1961), note 466, p. 162.

2. M. Cook, *The Koran: A Very Short Introduction* (New York: Oxford University Press, 2000), p. 117.

3. Ibid.

4. Ibid., p. 118.

5. T. Lester, "What is the Koran?" in *The Atlantic Monthly* (January 1999), p. 44.

6. A. Higgins, "The Lost Archive," in *The Wall Street Journal* (New York), January 12, 2008.

7. Gerd-R. Puin, "Observations on Early Qur'an Manuscripts in San`a," in Ibn Warraq (editor), *What the Koran Really Says* (Amherst, NY: Prometheus Books, 2002), p. 739.

8. Ibn Warraq, "Introduction," in *What the Koran Really Says* (Amherst, NY: Prometheus Books, 2002) pp. 59-60.

9. F. Braudel, *A History of Civilizations* (New York: Penguin Books, 1995), p. 22.

10. W.C. Smith, *On Understanding Islam* (Delhi: Idarah-I Adabiyat-I Delli, 1981), pp. 284-285.

11. Ali Abd al-Razik, "Islam and the Fundamentals of Authority: A Study of The Caliphate and Government in Islam" (Third Edition, 1344 A.H.; 1925 A.D.), p. 528. (Manuscript in English of Abd al-Razik's study submitted by Charles Clarence Adams as part of his doctoral dissertation to the University of Chicago, Chicago, Illinois, August 1928.)

12. M. Iqbal, *The Reconstruction of Religious Thought in Islam* (Lahore: Shaikh Muhammad Ashraf Publisher, reprint 1958), p. 165.

13. F. Rahman, *Islam* Second Edition (Chicago: University of Chicago Press, 1979), p. 31.

14. W.C. Smith, *What is Scripture? A Comparative Approach* (Minneapolis, MN: Fortress Press, 1993), p. 69.

15. Ibid., p. 89.

16. Ibid., p. 83.

17. Ibid., p. 89.

18. M. Iqbal, *The Reconstruction of Religious Thought in Islam*, p. 168.

19. M. Arkoun, *Rethinking Islam: Common Questions, Uncommon Answers* (Boulder, CO: Westview Press, 1994), p. 65; also see chapter 7 on "The Qur'an."

20. N.H. Abu Zayd, *Voice of an Exile: Reflections in Islam* (Westport, CT: Praeger Publishers, 2004), p. 57.

21. A. Soroush, *Reason, Freedom, and Democracy in Islam* (New York: Oxford University Press, 2000), p. 24.

22. F. Esack, *The Qur'an* (Oxford: Oneworld Publications, 2002), p. 12.

IV. The Qur'an Problem

1. See Pew Research Center, *The Future of World Religions: Population Growth Projections, 2010-2050*, April 2, 2015.

2. Octavio Paz, *One Earth, Four or Five Worlds: Reflections on Contemporary History* (New York: Harcourt Brace Jovanovich, 1985), p. 114.

3. Wilfrid Cantwell Smith, *What is Scripture? A Comparative Approach* (Minneapolis, MN: Fortress Press, 1993), p. 18.

4. For the ancient meaning of "theopolitics" see Yair Hoffmann, "Reflections on the relationship between Theopolitics, Prophecy and Historiography," pp. 85-99 in Henning Graf Reventlow, Yair Hoffmann and Benjamin Uffenheimer (editors), *Politics and Theopolitics in the Bible and Postbiblical Literature* (Sheffield: Sheffield Academic Press Ltd, 1994).

5. Arthur J. Arberry, *The Koran Interpreted* (London: Oxford University Press, 1964); verses quoted from the Qur'an are all from Arberry's rendition in English.

6. Friedrich Schleiermacher, *On Religion: Speeches to its Cultured Despisers* (New York: Harper & Row, 1958), p. 89.

7. M.A. Shaban, *Islamic History: A New Interpretation*, volume 1, A.D 600-750 (Cambridge, U.K.: Cambridge University Press, 1971), pp. 14-15.

8. Philip Jenkins, *Jesus Wars: How Four Patriarchs, Three Queens, and Two Emperors Decided What Christians Would Believe for the Next 1,500 Years* (New York: HarperCollins Publishers, 2010), p. 16.

9. Arnold J. Toynbee, *A Study of History*. Abridgement of Volumes I-VI by D.C. Somervell (New York, Oxford: Oxford University Press, 1946), pp. 488-489.

10. Cited by Abdus Salam (Nobel prize in Physics 1979) in "Renaissance of Sciences in Arab and Islamic Lands" in Z. Hassan & C.H. Lai (editors) *Ideals and Realities: Selected Essays of Abdus Salam* (Singapore: World Scientific Publishing Co Pte Ltd., 1984), p. 244.

11. Marshall G.S. Hodgson, *The Venture of Islam: Conscience and History in a World Civilization*, volume 1 (Chicago: The University of Chicago Press, 1974), p. 389.

12. Aristotle, *The Ethics of Aristotle: The Nicomachean Ethics.* Translated by J.A.K. Thomson (Harmondsworth, England: Penguin Books, Revised edition 1976), p. 333.

13. Michael Allen Gillespie, *The Theological Origins of Modernity* (Chicago: The University of Chicago Press, 2008), p. 22.

14. Ibid., p. 23.

15. Ernest Renan, *Islam and Science: A Lecture Presented At La Sorbonne* 29 March 1883. English translation by Sally P. Ragep (Montreal: McGill University, 2011), p. 7.

16. Cited in Majid Fakhry, *A History of Islamic Philosophy*, Second Edition (New York: Columbia University Press, 1983), p. 251.

17. Muhammad Abul Quasem (Translator), *The Jewels of the Qur'an, Al-Ghazali's Theory*. A translation, with an introduction and annotation of al-Ghazali's *Kitab Jawahir al-Quran* (London and New York: Kegan Paul International, 1983), pp. 26-27.

18. Ibn Al `Arabi, *The Bezels of Wisdom*. Translation and Introduction by R.W.J. Austin. (Mahwah, NJ : Paulist Press, 1980), p. 25.

19. See William C. Chittick, *Ibn `Arabi: Heir to the Prophets* (Oxford: Oneworld Publications, 2005).

20. Cited in Annemarie Schimmel, *I Am Wind, You Are Fire: The Life and Work of Rumi* (Boston & London: Shambala Publications, Inc., 1992), p. 115.

21. Annemarie Schimmel, *Mystical Dimensions Of Islam* (Chapel Hill, NC: The University of North Carolina Press, 1975), p. 318.

22. Fernand Braudel, *A History of Civilizations* (New York: Penguin Books, 1995), p. 41.

23. Abdelwahab Meddeb, *The Malady of Islam* (New York: Basic Books, 2003), p. 6.

24. Abdelwahab Meddeb, *Islam and the Challenge of Civilization* (New York: Fordham University Press, 2013), p. 80.

25. Sayyid Qutb, *Milestones* (New Delhi: Islamic Book Service, 2002), p. 35.

26. See, for instance, the biographical chapters on these three among other Muslim public figures in the history of modern India from the perspective of a sympathetic Hindu. Rajmohan Gandhi, *Eight Lives: A Study of the Hindu-Muslim Encounter* (Albany, NY: State University of New York Press, 1986).

27. Sayyid Qutb, *Milestones*, pp. 10-11.

28. Eric Ormsby, *Ghazali: The Revival of Islam* (Oxford: Oneworld Publications, 2008), p. ix.

29. Quoted in Eric Ormsby, *Ghazali: The Revival of Islam*, p. 128.

30. Wilfrid Cantwell Smith, *What is Scripture? A Comparative Approach*, p. 70.

31. *Al-Ghazzali's Mishkat Al-Anwar ("The Niche For Lights")*. A Translation With Introduction By W.H.T. Gairdner. Asiatic Society Monographs Vol. XIX. (London: Published by the Royal Asiatic Society, 1924), pp. 89-90.

V. Arab and Muslim AntiSemitism

1. B. Lewis, *The Jews of Islam* (Princeton, NJ: Princeton University Press, 1984), p. 85.

2. David J. Wasserstein, "So, what did the Muslims do for the Jews?" in *The Jewish Chronicle*, May 24, 2012.

3. See EU Agency for Fundamental Rights, *Discrimination and hate crime against Jews in EU Member States: experiences and perceptions of anti-Semitism*. November 2013.

4. Robert S. Wistrich, *Muslim Anti-Semitism: A Clear and Present Danger* (The American Jewish Committee, 2002).

5. See David Pollock, *Beyond Words: Causes, Consequences, & Cures for Palestinian Authority Hate Speech* (The Washington Institute for Near East Policy, 2013); available as pdf document at www.washingtoninstitute.org.

6. See, for instance, David D. Dalin and John F. Rothmann, *Icon of Evil: Hitler's Mufti and the Rise of Radical Islam* (New York: Random House, 2008).

7. Neil J. Kressel, *"The Sons of Pigs and Apes": Muslim Antisemitism and the Conspiracy of Silence* (Washington, D.C.: Potomac Books, 2012), p. 1.

8. Ibid., pp. 3-4.

9. Ibid., p.4.

10. Ibid.

11. See references to the Jews by Khomeini in *Islam and Revolution: Writings and Declarations of Imam Khomeini*. Translated and Annotated by Hamid Algar (Berkeley: Mizan Press, 1981).

12. Wistrich, op. cit., p. 4.

13. See B. Tibi, *Islamism and Islam* (New Haven: Yale University Press, 2012) p. 56.

14. Ibid., pp. 55-56.

15. Wistrich, op.cit., p. 5.

16. B. Lewis, "The New Anti-Semitism," in *The American Scholar*, Winter 2006.

17. B. Lewis, "The New Anti-Semitism," in *The New York Review of Books*, April 10, 1986.

18. See Clinton Bennett, *In Search of Muhammad* (London and New York: Cassell, 1998); also Tarif Khalidi, *Images of Muhammad: Narratives of the Prophet in Islam Across the Centuries* (New York: Doubleday, 2009).

19. Sigmund Freud, *Moses and Monotheism* (New York: Vintage Books, 1967), p. 118.

20. Geiger's monograph was translated into English by F.M. Young in 1896 in Bangalore, India, and published two years later. This same edition was re-issued as *Judaism and Islam* (New York: Ktav Publishing House, 1970).

21. Geiger, *Judaism and Islam*, p. 1.

22. See Gordon D. Newby, "The Jews of Arabia at the Birth of Islam," in Abdelwahab Meddeb and Benjamin Stora (editors), *A History of Jewish-Muslim Relations: From the Origins to the Present Day* (Princeton and Oxford: Princeton University Press, 2013), pp. 39-51.

23. Frithjof Schuon, *Understanding Islam* (Bloomington, Indiana: World Wisdom Books, Inc., 1994), p. 39.

24. Schuon, op. cit., pp. 40-41.

25. Dr. Tawfik Hamid, *Inside Jihad: How Radical Islam Works, Why It Should Terrify Us, How to Defeat It* (Mountain Lake Park, MD: Mountain Lake Press, 2015), pp. 157-158.

26. See Exodus (31:14), "Ye shall keep the sabbath therefore; for it is holy unto you: everyone that defileth it shall surely be put to

death: for whosoever doeth any work therein, that soul shall be cut off from among his people." *The Bible,* Authorized Version. Bible Society, Stonehill Green, Westlea, Swindon. Printed in Great Britain.

27. Muhammad Asad, *The Message of the Quran* (Bristol, England: The Book Foundation, 2003), p. 21, fn. 50.

28. See "Berlin to Makkah: Muhammad Asad's Journey into Islam," by Ismail Ibrahim Nawwab in the magazine *Saudi Aramco World,* pp. 6-32, January/February 2002.

29. See, for instance, W.N. Arafat, "New Light on the Story of Banu Qurayza and the Jews of Medina," in the *Journal of the Royal Asiatic Society of Great Britain and Ireland,* No. 2 (1976), pp. 100-107; and M.J. Kister, "The Massacre of the Banu Qurayza: A re-examination of a tradition," in *Jerusalem Studies in Arabic and Islam,* Vol. 8 (1986), pp. 61-96.

30. See Exodus, 32:26-28.

31. Freud, op. cit., p. 136.

32. See John Moorhead, "The Earliest Christian Theological Response to Islam," in *Religion* (1981), vol. 11, pp. 265-274. Also see *The Armenian History attributed to Sebeos.* Translated, with notes, by R.W. Thomson (Liverpool, UK: Liverpool University Press, 1999), pp. 95-96.

33. See Arafat, fn. 28.

34. Abdelwahab Meddeb, *Islam and the Challenge of Civilization* (New York: Fordham University Press, 2013), p. 14.

35. Asad, op. cit., p. 295, fn. 40.

36. See, for instance, Sadakat Kadri, *Heaven on Earth: A Journey Through Shari`a Law from the Deserts of Ancient Arabia to the Streets of the Modern Muslim World* (New York: Farrar, Straus and Giroux, 2012) pp. 99-105.

37. See Robert R. Reilly, *The Closing of the Muslim Mind: How Intellectual Suicide Created the Modern Islamist Crisis* (Wilmington, Delaware: ISI Books, 2010).

38. Meddeb, *Islam and the Challenge of Civilization*, p. 30.

39. Carl W. Ernst, *How to Read the Qur'an: A New Guide, with Select Translations* (Chapel Hill: The University of North Carolina Press, 2011) pp. 16-17.

40. See Asad, *The Message of the Qur'an*, footnote 87, p. 31.

41. Mahmoud Mohamed Taha, *The Second Message of Islam*. Translation and Introduction by Abdullahi Ahmed An-Na'im (Syracuse, NY: Syracuse University Press, 1987).

42. Sigmund Freud, *Civilization and Its Discontents* (New York & London: W.W. Norton & Co., 1961) p. 47.

43. See Sigmund Freud, *The Future of an Illusion* (New York & London: W.W. Norton & Co., 1961), pp. 7-8.

44. See Wilferd Madelung, *The succession to Muhammad: A study of the early Caliphate* (Cambridge: Cambridge University Press, 1997). Also see Lesley Hazleton's book based on early Muslim sources, *After the Prophet: The Epic Story of the Shia-Sunni Split* (New York: Random House, 2009).

45. Hazleton, op. cit., pp. 191-192.

46. Freud, *Moses and Monotheism*, pp. 116-117.

VI. ISIS, Saudia Arabia and the West

1. Adonis, *Violence & Islam: Conversations with Houria Abdelouahed* (Cambridge, UK: Polity Press, 2016), p. 37.

2. Philby mentioned only in passing the pillage of the Sharifian palaces, and destructions of the domed tombs of pious men or Muslim saints found in the two holy cities of Islam.

3. On Philby, see Elizabeth Monroe, *Philby of Arabia* (London: Faber and Faber, 1973).

4. H. St. John Philby, *Sa'udi Arabia* (New York: Frederick A. Praeger, 1955), pp. 290-291.

5. For a brief study on the subject see Hamid Algar, *Wahhabism: A Critical Essay* (Oneonta, NY: Islamic International Publications, 2002).

6. Algar, p. 10.

7. Philby, *Sa'udi Arabia*, p. 33.

8. Algar, p. 34.

9. H.A.R. Gibb, *Studies on the Civilization of Islam* (Boston: Beacon Press, 1962), p. 181.

10. See G.E. von Grunebaum, *Classical Islam: A History, 600 A.D. to 1258 A.D.* (New Brunswick, N.J.: Transaction Publishers, 1970).

11. Gibb, p. 182.

12. Philby, *Sa'udi Arabia*, 93.

13. Husayn bin Ali, is Sharif Husayn, whose son was Prince Feisal, alongside T.E. Lawrence. The Sharif family was Sunni, as were the Ottomans.

14. Philby, *Sa'udi Arabia*, xi.

15. S.K. Aburish, *The Rise, Corruption and Coming Fall of the House of Saud* (New York: St. Martin's Press, 1995), p. 24.

16. Aburish, p. 34.

17. Algar, p. 33.

18. J.R. Bradley, *Saudi Arabia Exposed: Inside a Kingdom in Crisis* (New York: Palgrave Macmillan, 2005), p. xi.

19. Y. Trofimov, *The Siege of Mecca: The Forgotten Uprising in Islam's Holiest Shrine and the Birth of Al Qaeda* (New York: Doubleday, 2007), p. 251.

20. Cited in Robert Lacey, *Inside the Kingdom: Kings, Clerics, Modernists, Terrorists, and the Struggle for Saudi Arabia* (Toronto: Penguin Canada, 2009), p. 72.

21. Monroe, *Philby of Arabia*, pp. 69-70.

22. See *Messages to the World: The Statements of Osama Bin Laden*. Edited and Introduced by Bruce Lawrence (London: Verso, 2005). For Bin Laden's letter to Sheik Bin Baz, see pp. 15-19.

23. On the making and spread of Islamism see, for instance, Richard P. Mitchell, *The Society of the Muslim Brothers* (New York: Oxford University Press, 1969, 1993); James Toth, *Sayyid Qutb: The Life and Legacy of a Radical Islamic Intellectual* (New York: Oxford University Press, 2013); Ibrahim M. Abu-Rabi', *Intellectual Origins of Islamic Resurgence in the Modern Arab World* (Albany: State University of New York Press, 1996); and Bassam Tibi, *Islamism and Islam* (New Haven: Yale University Press, 2012).

24. On Salafi, see the useful article by Bernard Haykel, "Salafis," in Gerhard Bowering (editor), *The Princeton Encyclopedia of Islamic Political Thought* (Princeton, NJ: Princeton University Press, 2013), pp. 483-84.

25. W.C. Smith, *Islam in Modern History* (Princeton, NJ: Princeton University Press, 1957), p. 68.

26. Sayyid Qutb, *Milestones* (New Delhi: Islamic Book Service, 2002), p. 76.

27. See R.P. Mitchell, *The Society of the Muslim Brothers*, p. 207.

28. *Messages to the World. The Statements of Osama Bin Laden*, p. 49.

29. J. Burke, *Al Qaeda: The True Story of Radical Islam* (London: I.B. Tauris, 2004), p. 182.

30. *Messages to the World. The Statements of Osama Bin Laden*, p. 111.

31. Ibid., pp. 247-248.

32. F. Ajami, "Reaping the whirlwind," in *U.S. News and World Report*, 28 June 2004.

33. L. Napoleoni, *The Islamist Phoenix: The Islamic State and the Redrawing of the Middle East* (New York: Seven Stories Press, 2014), p. 36.

34. K. Makiya, *Cruelty and Silence: War, Tyranny, Uprising, and the Arab World* (New York: W.W. Norton, 1993), p. 224.

35. Thomas E. Ricks, "Briefing Depicted Saudis as Enemies," in *Washington Post*, Tuesday 6 August 2002, p. A01.

36. Quoted in Patrick Cockburn, "Iraq Crisis: How Saudi Arabia helped Isis take over the north of the country," in *Independent* (UK), Saturday 12 July 2014.

37. Quoted in Michael Weiss and Hassan Hassan, *ISIS: Inside the Army of Terror* (New York: Regan Arts, 2015), p. 41.

VII. Islamism in the Rear-View Mirror

1. Z. Hassan & C.H. Lai (editors), *Ideals & Realities: Selected Essays of Abdus Salam* (Singapore: World Scientific Publishing, 1984), pp. 151-152.

2. E. Cleaver, *Soul on Ice* (New York: Dell Publishing, 1968), p. 61.

3. B. Lewis, "The Roots of Muslim Rage," in *The Atlantic Monthly* (September 1990), pp. 47-60.

4. For an English translation see Muhammad Iqbal, *Shikwa & Jawab-i-Shikwa: Complaint and Answer: Iqbal's Dialogue with Allah* translated from Urdu by Khushwant Singh (Delhi: Oxford University Press, 1981; reprint 1983).

5. M. Bennabi, *Islam: In History and Society* (Kuala Lumpur, Malaysia: Berita Publishing, 1991), p. 10.

6. Lewis, "The Roots of Muslim Rage."

7. In Indonesia and Malaysia in southeast Asia; in Pakistan, Afghanistan, Iran, Iraq, Syria, Jordan, Lebanon, Egypt in the greater Middle East; in Tunisia, Algeria, Morocco in North Africa; in Central Asian republics that were then under Soviet rule.

8. Adonis, *Violence & Islam: Conversations with Houria Abdelouahed* (Cambridge, UK: Polity Press, 2016), p. 76.

9. Lewis, "The Roots of Muslim Rage."

10. V.S. Naipaul, *Among the Believers: An Islamic Journey* (London: Andre Deutsch, 1981), p. 364.

11. E. Hobsbawm labeled the twentieth century the "Short Twentieth Century 1914-1991" for the sub-title of his book *Age of Extremes* (London: Little, Brown and Co., 1994). Similarly, J. Lukacs began his book *The End of the Twentieth Century* (New York: Ticknor & Fields, 1993) by stating, "It was a short century. It lasted seventy-five years – from 1914 to 1989."

12. F. Fukuyama, *The End of History and the Last Man* (New York: The Free Press, 1992), p. xx.

13. I. Babbitt, *Democracy and Leadership* (Indianapolis: Liberty Classics reprint, 1979), p. 23.

VIII. An Afterword

1. Fouad Ajami, "Islam's Nowhere Men," in *The Wall Street Journal*, May 10, 2010.

2. *Arab Human Development Report* 2016 (New York: United Nations Development Programme, 2016), p. 22.

Select Glossary

`ālim:	religious scholar, learned individual; (plural ulema).
Abbasid:	a ruling dynasty of the Caliphate c. 750-1258 C.E.
ahl al-kitab:	people of the book, traditionally meaning Jews and Christians.
amir al-mu'minīn:	commander, leader, head of the believers.
Ash`arî:	the main school of Sunni Islamic theology from medieval era to present, named after the early tenth century theologian Abul Hasan al-Ash`arî (d. 935).
bätin:	esoteric, inner, intrinsic, hidden meaning.
bid'āh:	innovation; in religion unorthodox innovation denounced as heterodoxy.
dār al-harb:	land of war.
dār al-Islam:	land, or house, of Islam.
falsafāh:	philosophy.
faqīh:	a Muslim jurisprudent; (plural fuqāha).
fiqh:	Islamic jurisprudence.
ghazzu:	armed raid.
hadīth:	words and deeds recorded of Prophet Muhammad; it is not the Qur'an, which is considered literally to be the Word of God.

halal:	lawful, permissible.
haram:	unlawful, forbidden, prohibited.
ijmā`	consensus.
ijtihād:	intellectual effort in reaching an independent judgment on a legal or theological question.
Imam:	an Islamic leader of congregational prayer in mosque; a holy or saintly individual; an honorific title.
insan:	human being.
jāhiliyyah:	state of ignorance; pre-Islamic era.
jihād:	the literal meaning being struggle, or effort; it has been traditionally and generally understood to mean holy war against infidels and apostates.
kalām	theology.
madrasāh:	school.
ma`sūm:	sinless, free from error, innocent.
mo'min:	a believer.
Mu`tazilî:	a rationalist school of theology in early Islam.
qiyās:	reasoning by analogy.
salaf:	the righteous ancestors, in particular referring to the first three generations of Muslims in Islamic history.

salafiyya:	the tendency or movement to revive the pristine Islam of the earliest era of the salaf.
Shariah:	Islamic law as codified during the classical period eighth through the twelfth century.
Shi`a:	the minority sect in Islam.
shîrk:	associating partner(s) with God; polytheism.
sira:	biography, especially of Prophet Muhammad.
Sufi:	devotee of the mystical tradition within Islam.
sunna:	practice, custom of Prophet Muhammad.
Sunni:	the majority sect in Islam.
takfīr:	the pronouncement or accusation by one Muslim of another Muslim to be an apostate or unbeliever; the Muslim making the accusation is referred to as *takfīri.*
taqlīd:	the principle of imitation or strict adherence to Shariah.
tariqāh:	in Sufi tradition and Sufi circles meaning the "path" or order or fraternity of the mystics.
taw'ba:	repentance.
Umayyad:	a ruling dynasty of the Caliphate c. 661-750 C.E.
ummah:	community.
zähir:	manifest, clear, present.

Suggested Readings

Arberry, Arthur J. *The Koran Interpreted.* London: Oxford University Press, 1964.

Arberry, Arthur J. *Sufism: An Account of the Mystics in Islam.* London: George Allen & Unwin, 1950.

Arkoun, Mohammed. *Rethinking Islam: Common Questions, Uncommon Answers.* Boulder, CO: Westview Press, 1994.

Asad, Muhammad. *The Message of the Quran.* Bristol, England: The Book Foundation, 2003.

Asad, Muhammad. *The Road to Mecca.* Gibraltar: Dar al-Andalus, 1981.

Ayoub, Mahmoud M. *Islam: Faith and History.* London: Oneworld Publications, 2004.

Berman, Paul. *Terror and Liberalism.* New York: W.W. Norton & Company, 2003.

Berman, Paul. *The Flight of the Intellectuals.* New York: Melville House Publishing, 2010.

Burckhardt, Titus. *An Introduction to Sufism.* London: Thorsons, 1995.

Donner, Fred M. *Muhammad and the Believers: At the Origins of Islam.* Cambridge, MA: Belknap Harvard University Press, 2010.

Eaton, Charles Le Gai. *Islam and the Destiny of Man.* Albany, NY: State University of New York Press, 1985.

Hamid, Tawfik. *Inside Jihad*. Mountain Lake Park, MD: Mountain Lake Press, 2015.

Hodgson, Marshall G.S. *The Venture of Islam: Conscience and History in a World Civilization* (3 volumes). Chicago, IL: the University of Chicago Press, 1974.

Khalidi, Tarif. *Images of Muhammad: Narratives of the Prophet in Islam Across the Centuries*. New York: Doubleday, 2009.

Lewis, Bernard. *The Crisis of Islam*. New York: Random House, 2004.

Lewis, Bernard. *The Jews of Islam*. Princeton, NJ: Princeton University Press, 1984.

Lewis, Bernard. *Faith and Power: Religion and Politics in the Middle East*. New York: Oxford University Press, 2010.

Meddeb, Abdelwahab. *Islam and the Challenge of Civilization*. New York: Fordham University Press, 2013.

Mernissi, Fatima. *Islam and Democracy: Fear of the Modern World*. Indianapolis, IN: Addison-Wesley Publishing Company, 1992.

Mitchell, Richard P. *The Society of the Muslim Brothers*. New York: Oxford University Press, 1969.

Momen, Moojan. *An Introduction to Shi`i Islam*. New Haven & London: Yale University Press, 1985.

Rahman, Fazlur. *Islam and Modernity: Transformation of an Intellectual Tradition*. Chicago, IL: The University of Chicago Press, 1982.

Rodinson, Maxime. *Mohammed*. Harmondsworth, UK: Penguin Books, 1971.